TEENS CAN MAKE IT HAPPEN WORKBOOK

STEDMAN GRAHAM

A Fireside Book

Published by Simon & Schuster

New York London Toronto Sydney Singapore

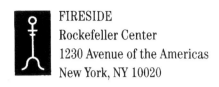

FIRESIDE
Rockefeller Center
1230 Avenue of the Americas
New York, NY 10020

For information about special discounts for bulk purchases,
please contact Simon & Schuster Special Sales:
1-800-456-6798 or business@simonandschuster.com

Designed by Ruth Lee

Manufactured in the United States of America

10   9   8   7   6   5   4   3   2

Library of Congress Cataloging-in-Publication Data is available.

ISBN: 978-0-7432-2558-8

Acknowledgments

The publication of my recent book, *Teens Can Make It Happen,* has brought me tremendous satisfaction, because it allows me to reach out to a population that is very important to our society: young people, people on the cusp of making major decisions that will affect how they grow and live and find meaning in their lives. That publication—a guide to teach young people the process for success—afforded me the opportunity to visit numerous schools and youth-serving organizations and talk with young people across the country, ranging from middle school on up. Those visits confirmed what I already knew: The young people of today possess unlimited potential and are a great source of inspiration and hope for tomorrow. Their response to the Success Process teachings has been both rewarding and encouraging.

Now that book has a companion, the *Teens Can Make It Happen Workbook*, which will make the material even more helpful to teens who are eager to make the most of their lives. The *Teens Can Make It Happen Workbook* is filled with a variety of activities and exercises that will help teens explore further each of the Nine Steps to Success detailed in the *Teens Can Make It Happen* book. These activities teach teens practical concepts for success *and* how to apply them in the real world. The content has been carefully developed to help teens get started on and sustain their journey through the Success Process. Yet again, every chapter shows that you are not your *circumstances*; you are your *possibilities*.

Yet again, I wish to thank the people who participated in our pilot programming at Shorewood High School in Shorewood, Wisconsin: teacher Lisa Bromley, educational consultant Linda D'Acquisto, and the wonderful group of students who worked tirelessly with us to adapt our Success Process teachings for youths.

My sincere thanks also go to my agent, Jan Miller, and to Shannon Miser-Marven for their steadfast support of my work. I would also like to acknowledge the incredible work done by my team at Simon & Schuster, particularly that of Carolyn Reidy, Dominick Anfuso, London King, and Kristen McGuiness.

Finally, my thanks go to Tom Hanlon and Christopher Evans for their continued contributions to my work.

To all the youth who dare to dream
And who take the steps to make it happen

Contents

The Success Process

The world is a collection of unlimited wealth and resources. Often, we limit our potential by moving in our own small circles because of our fears. If we change the way we view the world, there is nothing we cannot accomplish.

—Stedman Graham

What does success mean to you? To some it means a lot of money or prestige, a big house, a fancy car, an executive position. To others it means doing what they want to do: winning an award, earning a scholarship, mastering new skills. Others might define success in terms of how strong their relationships are with family and friends.

Success can mean a lot of things to a lot of people, and that's all right. To me, people are successful when they are fulfilling their own potential, expanding their horizons, not afraid to take risks, and continually growing. Success comes from knowing who you are and what you want to achieve, what your abilities are and how you can use them to live a fulfilling life—one in which your potential is fully tapped.

As a teenager, it is easy for me to dream about a successful future. However, I need to concentrate on realistic goals and achieve them step by step. Success doesn't happen overnight, and it is important to realize that at my age. However, I believe that if I work on accomplishing my goals, my dreams, or parts of them, will come true."

—Lana, age eighteen

Too many kids nowadays don't even know what their potential *is,* much less how to tap into it. And success requires both of those things to happen. It doesn't just happen on its own.

> **S**uccess comes from knowing who you are and what you want to achieve, what your abilities are and how you can use them to live a fulfilling life.

So how *do* you become successful? How do you discover your potential and learn how to tap into it?

By engaging in a process that helps you pursue your dreams and goals. By taking action. By understanding that what happens to you is not nearly as important as how you choose to react or respond to it. By creating a vision and a plan to make that vision happen. By taking risks—and knowing which risks to take. By making wise decisions.

There are a number of factors involved in becoming successful, and they are all part of the Success Process that I detailed in my book *Teens Can Make It Happen: Nine Steps to Success.* That book, along with this workbook, will help you begin the Success Process. It will help you envision what success means to you in terms of your relationships with others, your education and career goals, and your role within your community.

Success Circles

Like many people, I wasted a great deal of my life worrying about what others thought of me. I still struggle with that, even though I now realize that it doesn't matter what others think of me; what matters most is how I feel about myself and that I believe in the *possibilities* for my life.

You can't do much about what others say or think about you. You can only focus on those things that are within your control. The things that matter most to you and that you have the power to influence are contained in what I call your Success Circles. These circles are simply a way of helping you focus on the most important areas of your life when you undertake the Success Process. That focus helps you to grow and enrich your life.

Anyone can come up with a dozen or more such circles, but let's consider these basic three: Personal Development, Career, and Relationships.

1. *Personal Development* refers to how you want to develop as a person. Your development will affect not only you, but also the community around you, as you see opportunities to give back to your community.

2. By *Career* I mean the things you can do now to help yourself to the type of career you envision for yourself.

3. Finally, *Relationships* are critical at every stage of our lives; no person is successful in isolation.

So what goes into these Success Circles? Well, your circles might begin to shape up like this:

Personal Development

- Work through my Success Process materials to better know myself, my needs, and my desires
- Define what success and achievement mean for me
- Start jogging or working out regularly
- Volunteer at summer camp
- Take part in a walkathon

Career

- Be more consistent with homework
- Hook up with a study partner
- Get a summer job in the type of business that interests me (such as working as an aide in a hospital if you're interested in a medical field)
- Take more advanced courses in my area of career interest
- Take a variety of courses to expand my career opportunities
- Talk with and learn from people who are working in my area of career interest

Relationships

- Get along better with my parents
- Be more open in talking about things that are really bothering me
- Be supportive and encouraging to my close friends
- Get to know someone in my field of interest who can begin to "show me the ropes" (for instance, if you want to be a coach, choose a coach you want to model yourself after and strike up a relationship so you can begin to learn from him or her)
- Help my grandparents with house and yard work

The relationship circle is critical, for without consistent and strong relationships, it is difficult to build a meaningful life. Listen to what this student has to say about relationships and motivation:

> It may be possible for a short period of time, but in the long run I doubt anyone can find constant motivation from within. The quality of support for each person, I think, varies. However, it is always important to get a bit of encouragement, praise, or validation along the way. Otherwise you may start to question whether or not your work is going anywhere.
>
> —Kelly, age eighteen

Create Your Success Circles

Now take some time to fill in your own Success Circles. Within each one, try to list at least five things you can do to better your life.

Success Circles

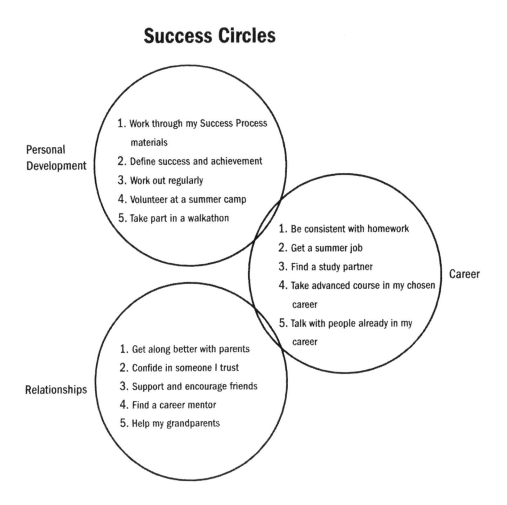

Personal Development

1. Work through my Success Process materials
2. Define success and achievement
3. Work out regularly
4. Volunteer at a summer camp
5. Take part in a walkathon

Career

1. Be consistent with homework
2. Get a summer job
3. Find a study partner
4. Take advanced course in my chosen career
5. Talk with people already in my career

Relationships

1. Get along better with parents
2. Confide in someone I trust
3. Support and encourage friends
4. Find a career mentor
5. Help my grandparents

If things aren't going well for you in one of these three areas—personal development, career, relationships—chances are it has a negative impact on the other areas. That's why it is so important to have a balanced life, to pay attention in equal measure to your schoolwork or your job if you have one, your personal development and the community around you, and your relationships with family, friends, and adults who are in positions to help you.

Also, note that often your circles will overlap. For example:

Success Circles

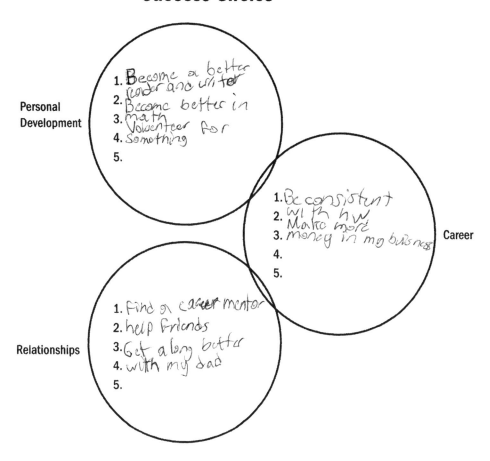

Personal Development

1. Become a better reader and writer
2. Become better in math
3. Volunteer for
4. Something
5.

Career

1. Be consistent with hw
2. Make more
3. money in my business
4.
5.

Relationships

1. Find a career mentor
2. help friends
3. Get along better
4. with my dad
5.

- Through an advanced class you're taking in your field of interest, a teacher might introduce you to someone in that field who could act as a mentor or guide.
- You might develop a key relationship while volunteering at a summer camp.
- Through an important relationship your eyes might be opened to an exciting career opportunity.

15

This overlapping strengthens your life in these key areas and gives you a more solid base from which to pursue a successful life.

THE EARLY STAGES OF LIFE

1-5 CHILDHOOD

5-13 ELEMENTARY SCHOOL

13-18 HIGH SCHOOL

18-22 COLLEGE OR VOCATIONAL TRAINING

22-25 FIRST JOB

25-30 DEVELOP REAL-WORLD KNOWLEDGE OF WORKFORCE

Steps to a Better Life

So what is this Success Process that I mentioned? The process involves nine steps. Following are brief descriptions of those steps.

- **Step 1: Check Your ID.** Self-awareness is where success begins. Before you can decide what you want for your life, you must first understand who you are, and why you think and act the way you do. Some describe this as searching for self-awareness. I call it "checking your ID." Before you take off on any serious journey these days, you must first make sure that you have valid identification with you. The same holds true for your journey through the Success Process.

- **Step 2: Create Your Vision.** To seek a better life, you have to decide what you want for your life. What are your dreams and aspirations? What characteristics, talents, and skills do you bring to the table? I'll help you explore these areas and then show you how to set ambitious but realistic goals.

- **Step 3: Develop Your Travel Plan.** Once you have established your goals, you need a plan to pursue your vision. In this step, I will help you develop that plan. I will also show you how to chart the best path by using your values as your markers.

- **Step 4: Master the Rules of the Road.** Every day you will encounter distractions that might stop you or slow you down in your journey. In step four, I will teach you how to "keep on keeping on." I will provide keys to self-motivation so that you will have the strength not to be easily distracted or defeated.

- **Step 5: Step into the Outer Limits.** There are always risks when you pursue a dream. To grow, you have to leave your comfort zone and enter unknown territory. Without taking those risks and facing your fears, you'll never get to where you want to be. You may fail sometimes, but you may *never* succeed if you are not willing to risk failure. And even if you do fail, you can learn from the experience and try again. To do that, you will need courage, and you will also need to have faith in your ability to achieve your goals.

- **Step 6: Pilot the Seasons of Change.** Many people never pursue their dreams for a better life because they are afraid of change, afraid they will lose something that has been important to them. But think about this: it is impossible to move ahead while staying where you are. You have to be willing to accept that some changes will be necessary. Many people keep doing the same thing over and over again in their lives, hoping that something better will come along. But if you keep doing what you have always done, you will get the same results. If you are not getting what you want out of life, you have to change your approach to it. Ride out the tough times and be patient for the changes you want to become real. Give yourself time to accept changes and adjust to them.

- **Step 7: Build Your Dream Team.** Supportive relationships that help you work toward your goals are critical to your success. To build those relationships, you need to learn to trust others. And to earn their trust, you in turn must be trust-worthy.

- **Step 8: Win by a Decision.** Making decisions wisely is one of your greatest challenges. This involves assessing your personal strengths, needs, and resources; checking them against your beliefs and values; and making decisions based on that assessment. You need a strong heart and a wise mind to do that.

- **Step 9: Commit to Your Vision.** In this final step, I will review all of the previous material with you and then teach you how to make a true commitment to achieving your vision for a successful life. You can set all the goals and make all the plans in the world, but unless you truly commit yourself to going after them, you'll never achieve them. You have to pursue your vision with energy and make that pursuit a priority in your life.

That's the Success Process in a nutshell. But to make it happen, you have to roll up your sleeves and get ready to do some work. Are you willing to do the work? It will be worth it, believe me. You'll get out of it what you put into it. If you want to get the most out of it, work carefully through the material and activities. Think seriously about how each step applies or should apply to how you live your life. In the end, what you take away from the nine-step Success Process is what matters most. Use it as a springboard to a promising future.

Now let's take the first step: let's check your ID.

Step 1: Check Your ID

There is something in every one of you that waits and listens for the sound of the genuine in yourself. It is the only true guide you will ever have. If you cannot hear it, you will all of your life spend your days on the ends of strings that somebody else pulls.

—Howard Thurman

You must believe in *possibilities*. It's unlikely that you'll lead a successful life if you don't believe that you have many possibilities. But you need more than that belief: you need to know who you are. Don't limit your possibilities, but pursue them according to *your* strengths, *your* desires, and *your* dreams. To do this you need to have strong self-awareness.

When you begin to focus on *your* possibilities, based on who *you* are, then those possibilities evolve from a generic "it's out there for everyone" idea into something that specifically reflects *your* personality, *your* strengths and dreams, *your* traits. In essence, you use this self-understanding, this self-awareness, to shape your vision for your life.

Do you know yourself? Life can be tough when you always feel that you have to prove yourself, that you're a victim of mistaken identity. Self-knowledge and self-

> To know yourself is the first, and most important, step in the process of pursuing your dreams and goals.

understanding are essential to pursuing a better life. So, in this step we'll explore the following:

- Knowing who you are and why you respond to certain people and situations in certain ways
- Using self-understanding as the cornerstone to building a successful life
- Overcoming obstacles and going through the sometimes-painful process of shedding your protective shell
- Replacing negative thoughts with positive thoughts
- Rescripting your life using the three C's: Confidence, Competence, and Capability

Defining Success

Success means different things to different people. Some people think success means a lot of money, a big house, a fancy car, or an executive position. Others think success means simply doing what they want to do. Think for a moment about what success means to you, and record your personal definition for success below.

I think success is to get a good job and to make money in it.

Validating Your ID: Knowing Who You Are

You can't open a bank account, drive a car, or get into a gym to attend a high school basketball game without showing valid identification. And you can't reach your full potential unless you also first validate your identity by knowing exactly who you are and where you want to go.

You have an invalid ID when you don't understand yourself or your actions: *Why did I get so upset when my parents didn't allow me to go to that party? Why am I so nervous around this boy or that girl?* You validate your identity when you come to understand yourself. You do that by learning what motivates you and flips your emotional switches.

Once you understand where your emotions and attitudes come from, then you can begin to understand not only why you act the way you do, but also why others see you the way they do. This knowledge gives you the power to change and control your behavior in a more positive and effective manner.

▣ Reality Check: Who Are You?

The first step in understanding who you are is to examine the things that influence your behavior. You'll do that in the following worksheet. This can be painful; it can mean confronting some serious issues and realities in your life. The poet and author Maya Angelou, who has not had an easy life, once said, "Success is not fame or fortune. It is picking up that burden and keeping on walking and not letting the pain trip you up."

Describe your five best features or characteristics: What do you like about yourself? Are you hard-working? Kind? Thoughtful? Serious? Fun-loving? Honest? Reliable? Realize that sometimes your *best* features may be hidden; they may not be your most obvious features. Think about and choose the features that describe you at your *best*:

1. I am Active
2. I am Healthy
3. I am Thoughtful
4. I am Kind
5. I am Reliable

Who are the types of people you most admire? Why?

I should Admire people that ~~are working~~ bilieve in things That I believe in.

If you could be like anyone, who would it be? Why?

I would be soccessful so my life would bccome easier

What makes you happy? Why?

Nice weather makes me happy because I love outdoor activity.

What makes you sad? Why?

Books movies and some tv shows.

What are the three things you are most afraid of? Why?

Bugs, being alone, and creeps

How have your fears influenced any decisions in your life?

What are three characteristics that may be holding you back from being more successful in your life?

My willingness to learn, my unpatientness, and my thinking

What experiences have caused you to develop these characteristics?

_____

_____

_____

What has been the biggest challenge in your life so far?

Overcomeing Fears.

_____

_____

_____

_____

When you are faced with a challenge, what is your typical reaction?

My reaction with a chalange is to overcome or figure out a way around it.

_____

_____

_____

Take a look one year down the road. What kind of person do you see yourself being? Imagine that you see yourself walking down a hallway. Describe yourself—not just in physical terms, but in terms of the features and talents that are beginning to shine.

_____

_____

_____

_____

_____

23

Building Success Through Self-Understanding

To know yourself is the first and most important step in the process of pursuing your dreams and goals. You need to become secure enough in who you are to accept the influence that others have on you. If you aren't secure in yourself, odds are you won't be open to the love, constructive criticism, and suggestions of those around you.

▪ Family Ties

This next activity will help you to focus on special strengths and qualities that are present in your family—as well as on your own special strengths and qualities.

Picture your favorite relative—the one you most enjoy seeing at holiday gatherings. List at least four specific characteristics of that person that help to explain why he or she is your favorite relative.

1. _Red hair_
2. _blue eyes_
3. _tall_
4. _Stylish_

Now, reverse roles. Ask that favorite relative to tell you at least four specific characteristics of yours that make you special. (This may involve a long-distance call!)

1. _____
2. _____
3. _____
4. _____

Now, reflect upon the following questions and write your answers in the spaces provided.

After speaking with your favorite relative, is there anything you would like to change about yourself?

_____
_____
_____
_____

Do you agree with what your relative said?

_____

_____

_____

_____

Was there anything your favorite relative said that surprised you?

_____

_____

_____

_____

What other characteristics would you like that relative to see in you, which may not be evident at this point in your life?

_____

_____

_____

_____

What characteristics that may not be evident at this point in your life would you like your favorite relative to see in you in the future?

_____

_____

_____

_____

Overcoming Obstacles

We all have obstacles to overcome. They come in all shapes and sizes: racism, sexism, and elitism are some big ones. Others are, so to speak, closer to home. You want to be a star athlete, maybe a professional athlete someday, but your athletic abilities are only average. You want to be taken seriously, for your thoughts and opinions to be valued, but you have a reputation as someone who's always joking around and so no one listens to you.

25

> **P**art of knowing who you are is understanding the obstacles you face and understanding how to get around those obstacles so that your gifts and abilities can flourish.

Part of knowing who you are, then, is understanding the obstacles you face and understanding how to overcome those obstacles so that your gifts and abilities can flourish. It's quite common to put a protective shell around yourself when you face a serious obstacle. You rationalize the problem or try to hide what you or others perceive as a shortcoming or a flaw. But that's not *overcoming* an obstacle; that's avoiding it—and in doing so allowing it to negatively impact your life. You need to change your way of thinking. Don't shrink from your obstacle. Face it and consider it in a new light.

Thinking Positively

To be successful, you should feel free to go after what you want in life. How do you do that? You become a positive, energized person. You don't think poorly of yourself or have a negative attitude. You get rid of negative baggage that holds you back. You believe in yourself—and when you believe in yourself, you give others reason to believe in you, too.

Vision is seeing your purpose in life, picturing who you are and what you're about and how you spend your time and energy. It's also about how you pursue your dreams and how you use your talents and abilities in that pursuit.

When your vision focuses on your potential and possibilities rather than on your past and limitations, then you can be helped by others and help them in return. To gain focus, though, sometimes you first have to get a grip on the feelings and beliefs that have held you back and limited your sense of who you are before you can move forward.

When you think more positively, you become more confident. This in turn helps you to feel more competent and capable. You see your negative thoughts in a different light: You realize that you used to automatically agree with whatever others would say about you, whether positive or negative. The negative thoughts were not only painful; many of them were wrong. Believing negative and false statements about yourself is like putting shackles on your legs and then wondering why you can't run.

▨ Turning Obstacles into Opportunities

What has been the most negative influence on your life? Why?

Parent's divorce beause it made my life harder and more complicated.

How has that negative influence affected your self-perception and behavior?

It has just made me more depressed and more challenged in some ways.

Part of being successful is turning negative influences into learning experiences and opportunities for growth. Have you been able to do this? If so, how? If not, how do you think some people are able to turn negatives into positives?

It is easy for some people beause they have many doulde with worse situations ohce know how to deul with the other ones.

What are some obstacles or personal flaws that keep you from being the "real you," or that keep you from doing what you want to do or being what you want to be?

27

What are ways around your obstacles? Don't fall into the trap of thinking there is no way around them. It may take some time or other people's help, but there is *always* a way around—or through or under or over—any obstacle.

Avoiding them pushing them away or just dealing with them.

What areas of your life are most difficult to share with others? Are there areas or issues that you're protective of or secretive about? Why?

If you were more vulnerable to family and close friends, if you were able to talk about some of these difficult issues or concerns, what do you think would happen?

It could either make or break our relationship if I was more open with my feelings

How can opening up and coming out of your protective shell help you on your road to living a more successful life?

It can open you to new successful people or gie you good idea

Rescript Your Life Using the Three C's

If you can understand who you are and where you want to go, if you can believe in the possibilities for your life, and if you feel like you deserve your dreams and goals, you are well on your way in the Success Process.

To be successful you must have the "three C's": confidence, competence, and capability.

Confidence

You must believe in yourself and feel worthy of your vision. You have to feel that you deserve success. You gain confidence by concentrating on your talents, accomplishments, and personal history—the things that make you special and unique.

Competence

We are all competent in different areas. As you become more competent at a variety of things, you begin to build not only skills, but an attitude that you, at your core, are a competent person. This is an invaluable attitude to have in your pursuit of success.

Capability

Capability is about a "can-do" attitude. It's one that is charged with energy, because you know you can do something. You must feel capable of defining, creating, and controlling your own life. After you attain small goals, you can work up to bigger ones, proving to yourself and others that you have the power to control your life—that you are capable.

Chances are, you'll feel confident, competent, and capable if you have a strong support system around you. Having relationships that strengthen you is vital. For many of us, that support begins with our family, but it can also come from others—friends, teachers, coaches, guidance counselors, and clergy, for instance. Such a support system helps you feel good about yourself and helps you focus on your strengths and gifts. People with positive self-images believe in themselves and in their abilities to control their own lives.

On the other hand, if you feel that you have little or no value, chances are you do not feel worthy of success. Perhaps you do not feel as though you deserve to have your deepest needs and desires recognized or realized. When this happens, your vision becomes severely limited, your life a self-fulfilling prophecy. You live down to low expectations rather than up to high expectations.

You need to stop accepting the limitations others have placed on you. Instead, start to believe in the *possibilities* for your life. You can, in essence, *rescript* your life, focusing on the areas you're competent and capable in.

■ Noting Your Talents and Achievements

When are you most confident? Why? List five situations or areas in which you feel confident.

I am confident in (or when) . . .

Sports

I am confident in (or when) . . .

School

I am confident in (or when) . . .

My house

I am confident in (or when) . . .

My Job.

I am confident in (or when) . . .

My old business.

Now, list five areas that you feel competent in, based on your experience. The items you list can be in broad areas such as academics, sports, or music, or they can be in skills or situations, such as being a loyal friend, a good listener, an encourager, an understanding person, and so on.

I am competent in (or at) . . .

School.

I am competent in (or at) . . .

Sports

I am competent in (or at) . . .

My house

I am competent in (or at) . . .

buisness

I am competent in (or at) . . .

at. encouraging

What are your capabilities? List five things you are capable of being or doing.

I am capable of (or at) . . .

completing School

I am capable of (or at) . . .

doing good in sports

I am capable of (or at) . . .

making money

I am capable of (or at) . . .

being successful

I am capable of (or at) . . .

being compassonal.

Next, think about what makes you feel good about yourself.

What are some of your proudest achievements?

My business altho it only lasted for aweek or two it was fun and exciting.

Why did they make you proud?

It made me proud because I made lots of money.

Based on your achievements, what do you think you are capable of doing in the next two to five years?

I could probably get a chance to get a bigger job.

In thinking of your competencies or talents, which ones give you the greatest pleasure?

I love being athletic it is fun and helpful in many ways

Which ones do you think you'd most like to continue to use and grow in during the next five years?

I would like to be and get more athletic

When you're *not* feeling confident or competent or capable, what are things you might do or thoughts you might have that can help you turn a negative into a positive?

You could look at the brighter side of the situation.

If you had trouble filling out these worksheets, don't feel bad. It's more a result of your not knowing yourself well enough yet than your not having any capabilities to speak of. Remember that we all are flawed—but that we also all have gifts to develop and to share. As you learn to know and accept yourself, you will find that it doesn't matter so much how other people treat you or perceive you. You will find that you are far less reactive to their perceptions of you and are more forgiving and accepting of both your flaws and weaknesses and those of people around you. You will begin to be far more dynamic in pursuing a better life for yourself and those you care about.

As you consider pursuing that rewarding life, the next chapter presents a most crucial step: creating your vision. How important is having a vision? The Bible puts it rather succinctly: where there is no vision, the people perish. The flip side of this states that *with* a vision, you yourself, and those around you, can prosper.

Step 2: Create Your Vision

We need to remember that we are created creative and can invent new scenarios as frequently as they are needed.

—Maya Angelou

Sometimes you hear that people "stumble into success," that they got there by "blind luck." I don't agree with these statements. People may come upon an opportunity that surprises them; something might open up for them without any of their planning or doing. But the people who *take* those opportunities and *make* something of them are the ones who are successful. And they are successful because they have a vision for what they can *do,* for what they can *be,* given that opportunity that they've come across.

So, you can create your vision beforehand, with careful thought and planning, or you can create it as you come upon new opportunities. But either way, to be successful, to seize those opportunities, you need to create your vision, because even if you know enough to answer when opportunity knocks, you can't sustain success for long without that vision.

Vision can begin with desire, but it doesn't end there. You can't just *want* something for yourself; you have to have a clear vision of how to *get* it. It's easy enough to dream about a better future for yourself, but you have to go beyond that. In this step of the Success Process, we'll help you create your vision as we examine what it means to:

- Have a vision for your life
- Decide where you want to go
- Create your vision step by step

In so doing, you'll learn to use your dreams to fuel your vision, and you'll learn to set goals, stay focused, and enjoy the journey.

Having a Vision for Your Life

As a teenager, I had the distractions that all kids face, but I stayed out of trouble because my parents let me know that they expected more of me. Gang membership held no allure for me—I had better things to look ahead to. In those years, I had a vision of getting an athletic scholarship to college and going on to professional basketball. That vision kept me on track.

Those who choose the way of the street do so because they have a limited vision of where their lives can go. Kids don't join gangs because they don't want to be doctors or computer analysts or teachers or actors or businesspeople. They join gangs because that is all they see for themselves. Their vision for their lives is severely limited.

Yet even if it doesn't lead to gang membership or crime, the lack of a vision for where you want to go in life hurts your growth as a person. Remember how we defined "vision" earlier? It's seeing your purpose in life, what you can *envision* yourself doing with your talents and desires. It is difficult to be successful if you have no vision or if you don't feel worthy of success. Having a vision for your life allows you to live out of hope rather than fear. In the next worksheet, we'll begin to look at the issues that will help you create your vision. Your vision will begin to emerge as you think about what you most enjoy doing and what talents you most enjoy using.

> Having a vision for your life allows you to live out of hope rather than fear.

▪ **Building on Pleasures and Talents**

What do you like doing most? Why?

I like working and helping others in and out of school.

What gives your life meaning? When do you feel most energized, alive?

I feel most energized in sports because I get excited and anxous to play and have fun

In a worksheet in the previous step (pages 31–32), you noted areas where you feel competent and capable. Refer back to that worksheet and then list five talents that you enjoy using.

1. _Sports_
2. _intelligence_
3. _Selling_
4. _creating_
5. _making $_

Now select the single talent that either is your best or is most important to you. Don't worry if you feel that you haven't "perfected" that talent; you have the rest of your life to keep improving it. This talent is central to your goals. If you have two talents that are really important to you, simply choose one over the other for the sake of this exercise. That doesn't mean you won't develop the other talent, too.

Write your best or most important talent(s) here:

Making money, selling, and creating.

Think about the many ways that you can use that talent, or those couple of talents, to improve your life. List ten ways that you can use your talent to improve your Success Circles (Personal Development, Career, and Relationships, or other areas of importance to you). Include things you are already doing with this talent, and add things you can envision yourself doing in the future as you grow that talent.

1. Making money
2. being successful
3. helping others
4. Making decisions
5.
6.
7.
8.
9.
10.

If You Could See Me . . . Then!

On this worksheet, focus on your vision. Here you'll explore issues that will help you shape your vision.

Begin to create your own vision by answering the following questions.

What is it that you enjoy doing most? What gives your life meaning?

I like playing sports and selling things to other people.

Being as specific as possible, describe what you will be doing in five years.

I will be graduating highschool hopefully with lots of money and a car.

_____

_____

_____

Identify two people who will be important to you as you pursue your vision. (Describe them but omit their names!)

1. _My mom because she helps me with decisions_

2. _Jack Nye because he gives me ideas and new interests._

What would you most like to do with your life if you didn't have to worry about money?

I would like a nice house a dog nice car family and places to go and enjoy

_____

_____

_____

Deciding Where You Want to Go

There's a saying that goes something like this: "If you don't know where you want to go, you'll probably end up someplace else." Once out of school, the average person changes careers—not just jobs within the same field—several times before settling in. Why? Because most people don't really know what they want to do with their lives.

Think of people you know who seem to be truly happy with their lives. I'll bet that they are doing what they want to do, living within the vision they chose for their lives. This is what Stephen Covey, author of _The 7 Habits of Highly Effective People_, refers to as beginning with the end in mind. If you know where you want to go, you can start your journey with confidence and purpose.

▪ Seeing the End Before You Begin

Describe a time when you began something with an end in mind. Did having the end in mind—in other words, the goal—help you? How?

Having a goal helps you become more successful in life and

Describe a time when you got into trouble or when you performed poorly in something because you didn't consider the end—your goal—but just plunged headlong into it. How might things have been different if you'd had the end in mind?

On tests sometimes I don't study and when I don't study it can sometimes give you a not so good grade.

Students who excel in school and life take responsibility for their lives. That is, they "take care of business" in the areas that are important to their success. In academics, that means studying for however long it takes to learn and know the material. In sports, it means taking extra batting practice in baseball or shooting fifty free throws after basketball practice is over. In music, it means practicing over and over until the music becomes part of you and flows naturally from you. Being responsible means knowing what your goal is and then taking the steps to make sure you reach your goal.

What are ways that you take responsibility for your life?

I take responsibility at school and at home for my poor actions

How does taking responsibility help you get where you want to go?

It will help you get to where you need/want to go because responsibility will make your life easier if you follow the rules and expectations.

Creating Your Vision, Step by Step

In the rest of this step of the Success Process we'll take you through six key steps of creating your vision:

- Taking inventory
- Using your imagination

- Setting goals
- Identifying role models and mentors
- Staying focused
- Enjoying the journey

Step One: Take Inventory

What gives meaning and joy to your life? How can you find a way to make your life an expression of that joy? Your talents are your gifts. When you express those gifts, the world opens up to you. If you develop your talents, people and resources will come to you. And I believe that the true meaning of success is using your talents and abilities—your gifts—to better not only your life, but the lives of those around you.

Many people think that a talent has to be so pronounced that it hits them over the head. If none does, they say, "I don't have any talents." The truth, however, is that often, you express your talents so naturally that you may not recognize them. What you love to do is generally what you naturally do well and what you have been doing all your life.

▪ Thinking on Purpose

Ask yourself what it is that you enjoy doing most. What gives your life meaning?

Helping others and playing with friends

Why do you think this activity is so meaningful to you?

It gives me joy and helps me live a better life

What do you look forward to doing more than anything else?

Sometimes spending time alone to just do whatever.

What is it that you would do with your life even if you didn't get paid for it?

Work at an aquarium

Step Two: Use Your Imagination

So far, you've begun to focus on the talents and interests you want to pursue. What next? You do what a child does during play: you use your imagination to create your reality.

Should you fantasize about finding a pot of gold on your doorstep? No. Fantasies are frivolous dreams. They can be fun, but they are dangerous if you spend so much time fantasizing that you neglect reality. Focus on dreaming within the realm of your experience. If you're planning to major in accounting in college, it does little good for you to fantasize about becoming a multimillionaire as soon as you graduate. Why? Because you're fantasizing about the goal without envisioning the process. It is far better to imagine the steps you'll need to take, from high school graduate to college student to college graduate to certified public accountant and on through the executive or entrepreneurial ranks.

Grownups, particularly athletes and artists, refer to this as the "visualization process." Great quarterbacks say that they can "see" the proper receiver get open and catch a pass before it is even thrown. Artists talk about visualizing a finished work before they have even begun it. Dreaming is different from fantasizing. To dream is to envision the possibility of something that is not only desirable, but attainable, based on who you are and where you can go in life. By allowing yourself to dream within that context, you can create a new reality and new possibilities for your life.

> To dream is to envision the possibility of something that is not only desirable, but attainable, based on who you are, and where you can go in life.

▪ Imagine That!

In earlier worksheets and exercises you've explored the areas in which you're confident, competent, and capable; the talents you most enjoy using and ways to grow those talents; beginning with the end in mind; and what gives your life meaning. Those exercises lead naturally to this one, where you draw on that understanding of yourself to create your vision.

Based on your talents and interests and what you find meaningful, what are some career fields (such as engineering, education, athletics, business, and so on) that you are considering? List as many choices as you want, and beside each choice write what is most attractive to you about that choice.

_____

_____

_____

_____

_____

_____

_____

_____

_____

_____

_____

If you listed more than three fields, what are your top three?

1. _____

2. _____

3. _____

Based on what you said in response to the question about what it is that you would do even if you didn't get paid for it, choose one field from your top three and circle it. This field should have possibilities in it for you that would allow you to do that one thing. List jobs or areas in that field that you would be interested in pursuing.

_____

_____

_____

Knowing yourself as you do, especially after having worked through preceding exercises and worksheets, complete the following sentence, from the gut level, without overanalyzing yourself.

If I could really do whatever I wanted in life, I would be a . . .

_____

_____

_____

Realize that this exercise doesn't limit you to one career field or choice; these decisions will evolve as you develop and grow as a person. This worksheet is meant to help you begin to consider your possibilities. Use it as a guidepost for now. In the next section we'll talk about goals—and how you have to be flexible in adapting them as you go along.

Step Three: Setting Goals

Once you have developed your vision, set goals to serve as stepping stones toward fulfilling your vision. Goals help you focus on where you want to be at each step of your journey so that as you proceed you can determine your progress toward fulfilling your vision.

As you set goals, keep these eight guidelines in mind:

1. **Goals should be realistic.** Don't waste your time setting unrealistic goals. You don't reach unrealistic goals—and then you feel discouraged, thinking you've failed. What you've really failed at is setting realistic goals.

2. **Goals should be meaningful.** Focus your goals on your vision. Don't set goals that lead you nowhere in particular. If you set goals that have no real meaning for your life, you may not achieve those goals—and even if you do, they won't get you closer to living the type of life that is truly meaningful to you.

3. **Goals should be well defined.** When you set out on a trip, you don't generally say, "Sometime soon, I think I'll go a couple hundred miles to the northeast somewhere and get there when I get there." No, you set a specific destination and a specific time when you want to be there. When you set goals in your journey to a better life, you want them to be just as well defined.

4. **Goals should excite YOU.** I put the emphasis on *you* because this is *your* vision for *your* life. People around you may have good intentions and you should certainly listen to and consider their advice, but don't let them throw you off the path by allowing them to set goals for you that are more in line with their vision than yours.

5. **Goals should follow a logical progression.** This is the old don't-put-the-cart-before-the-horse warning. Your goals should go step by step so they make perfect sense and so that you always know, out of pure logic, that the next one is within reach and that attaining it moves you toward your destination.

6. **Goals may need fine tuning.** Realistically, things can happen and circumstances can change as you pursue your vision of a better life, so your goals may require fine tuning along the way. You may accomplish some goals more easily than you had thought; others may elude you. Keep your vision in mind and adjust as you go to stay on target.

   The teen years, as you know, are times of turbulent change. Expect change to happen, expect your feelings and interests to change, and adjust your goals accordingly. The important thing is to keep goals ahead of you at all times. Goals are not the ultimate reward. The reward is in pursuing the dream.

7. **Goals should require positive action.** A primary purpose for setting goals is to get you moving in the right direction. There is really no reason to set goals that don't challenge you to take action. "I am going to consider losing some weight" is not a goal. By contrast, "At ten A.M. tomorrow I am going to jog three miles" is a goal. Setting goals within each of your Success Circles, acting upon them, and achieving them not only moves you forward, but it builds your confidence in your ability to pursue your vision of a better life. Goals help you act on your dreams rather than just wishing or hoping for them.

8. **Goals should not isolate you.** I know of a very smart person whose goal was to become a surgeon. He set his mind on that goal in high school and went after it. But he became so obsessed with his goal that he neglected most of the rest of his life. He never formed close relationships because they might have distracted him from his studies. He rarely went to family functions because he didn't want to fall behind in school.

   He reached his goal of becoming a surgeon, but now he has no life outside of his work, and so his life is one-dimensional. He is a lonely guy because while he took care of business, he didn't take care of the rest of his life. Your relationships and your personal life are not secondary considerations. Goals should not be all consuming and focused on one aspect of life; they should be part of a healthy life, addressing many aspects, helping you to be a more complete person.

You may come from a disadvantaged background. You may have low self-esteem. But you are free to dream of a better life and then to act upon that dream. There will be challenges in life; we all have our challenges. If you are going nowhere, there is no reason to take on those challenges, but if you have goals and a vision of where you want to go, then you will be motivated to overcome the challenges. You may not overcome every challenge, but if you learn from each of them and hold on to your vision, it is almost impossible to be defeated.

▪ Goals: The Game Plans of Life

For goals to be effective, they need to be built around some guiding principles—your values and beliefs. What values, beliefs, or principles matter most to you?

_____

_____

_____

The following list of values may help you identify your values or beliefs. Circle those that are meaningful to you.

achievement	health	possessions
aesthetics	helping	power
appearance	home	prestige
beauty	honesty	purpose
career achievement	influence	recognition
creativity	intimacy	security
dependability	justice	self-direction
education	knowledge	self-respect
enjoyment	leisure	self-determination
financial security	meaning	sharing
friendship	new experiences	status
genuineness	physical comforts	travel
growth	pleasure	wealth

The Pope has goals; so does a car thief. The difference is in the quality of their vision and their focus. Go over the following questions when considering how your vision is going to be focused.

What do you want to accomplish in your life?

I want to accomplish lots of money and success and happyness

_____

_____

_____

_____

Why do you want to achieve your goals? For example, will society or people around you benefit?

Some people will be helpful and others want
but you just have to keep on track

Make a list of ten goals that will help you pursue your vision. Your goals should be in line with your talents and your values.

1. _Graduate Middle school_
2. _Graduate Highschool_
3. _Graduate College_
4. _Get a car_
5. _Save money_
6. _get to work on time everyday_
7. _buy a house_
8. _Help at home_
9. _Save enough money to have a family_
10. _buy a pet dog_

Setting Goals

A vision statement is the big picture. Goals are pieces of the bigger picture—pieces of the puzzle, if you will. When you reach your goals, the bigger picture begins to take shape. This activity will help you continue to shape the goals that are important to you.

To achieve your vision you must have goals that act as guideposts along the way. Those goals will keep you focused and allow you to measure your success as you work toward making your vision a reality.

Now write some goals.

Write one goal for *tomorrow* that takes into account your Success Circles and your vision.

Continu to work on this work book and or complete allchecklist choores.

Write one goal for *next week* that takes into account your Success Circles and your vision.

Do my checklist everg day and remember everything I need to remember.

Write one goal for *this school year* that takes into account your Success Circles and your vision.

Get a A- or higher on a test.

Write five *long-term goals* that take into account your Success Circles and your vision.

1.
2.
3.
4.
5.

Step Four: Identifying Role Models and Mentors

49

A role model is someone whom you admire and would like to model parts of your life after. Sometimes a role model is someone you know—a parent, a brother or sister, an aunt or uncle, a teacher or coach, and so on. Sometimes a role model is someone you don't know personally, but know enough about his or her life that you aspire to be like him or her.

A mentor, on the other hand, is an adult who acts as a trusted counselor or guide. Mentors not only can help you establish goals and pursue them, but they can offer you advice and encouragement along the way.

■ A Little Help from Your Mentors and Role Models

Make a list of the people who have helped you and how they have helped. (*Example: Coach Smith always worked hard and was considerate to everyone.*)

Mom always tells me to do the right thing

Coach Libo helps me have good mindset

and determination

If you can't think of anyone, your problem may be that you have not clearly defined your vision for your life. Remember, you can't expect others to see it for you if you can't see it for yourself.

Now make a list of up to five people who could provide wisdom, guidance, and encouragement as you set goals. Make specific plans for contacting these people and for seeking their guidance.

1. Mom
2. Jack
3. Coach Libo
4. Wine - Counselor
5. John Salt

Consider the area or field in which you'd like to be mentored. What type of advice are you seeking?

Coaching jobs I want to be a better coach and or better

In your relationship with a mentor, what are your responsibilities? That is, given that he or she is there to help you, what can you do to help your mentor help you?

I need to be willing to practice the homework or be open to everything.

How can you get the most out of a relationship with a mentor, while not taking advantage of the mentor's time?

I can stay focused with the mentor doing what he asks of me.

Step Five: Staying Focused

Setting goals is one thing; staying focused on them is another—and often harder—thing to do. To be successful, you have to follow through and stay focused in life. If not, you lose power and direction. It's not that you can't enjoy other aspects of your life, but those goals always have to be at the forefront. Successful people are focused and not easily distracted from their goals, whatever those goals are.

Step Six: Enjoying the Journey

As you work toward your goals, if you find yourself anxious and snapping at people, it may be a warning that you've wandered off track or perhaps that your vision needs adjustment. Remember, this is a long journey, a life's journey, and you want to be able to savor and enjoy each step along the way.

Your Vision Statement

The preceding exercises and activities have covered a variety of issues that will help you shape your own vision. Here you get the opportunity to write your Vision Statement—the statement that will act as a rudder guiding your actions.

Picture a tall pine tree—ninety feet tall. Imagine that each foot of that tree represents one year in your life. The tree has a strong root system, one that reaches far underground. The roots keep the tree stable, alive, and growing under all conditions.

Your Vision Statement is much like the tree's root system. It will keep you standing and growing strong. Whatever life throws in your direction, you will have the stability to deal with the change. Notice that the period of being a teenager is only seven years long—yet it is critical in building a strong trunk to support the remaining years of your life.

In the space provided, compose a Vision Statement that takes into account your Success Circles, your definition for success, your strengths, interests, and dreams.

Know that some Vision Statements are long, some are short. Some are poems, some are songs, some are declarations. Some people weave their favorite quotations into their vision statement. There is no right or wrong way to build a personal Vision Statement. Ask yourself when you are finished, "Am I inspired by my Vision Statement? Does it capture what is truly meaningful to me?" If so, you are on the right track. If not, take more time to think about your vision. After all, it's your life's blueprint.

▪ MY VISION STATEMENT:

I see myself in a couple of years going to college or working at a resturant. I Dont know what I'm going to be but I will find the perfect job for me when I get there.

I see myself in a couple of years working at a restaurant or going to college. I Dont know what I'm going to be but I will figure that out later in life.

▨ A Look in the Rearview Mirror

This final activity engages your imagination, much as the vision exercises have. But this one has a twist: here you are imagining yourself looking *back* on your life to see what you have accomplished. This will help you shape your vision from a slightly different perspective.

You are now fifty years old and are getting ready to write your autobiography. Write the introduction for your autobiography here. In this introduction, include:

what name 3

- A summary of your life
- The key people who have helped you along the way
- Your training and educational accomplishments related to your goal statements
- Your achievements as they relate to your Success Circles and your Vision Statement

> As a child I always was active and ~~excited~~ excited for what was to come, but some (challanges) found me, what I did was simply solve them on my own I was allways very independant and relied on myself for guidance. In middle school I ~~accled~~ excelled in all classes and I learned much and ~~made~~ made many great friends. As I grew up I kept ~~becoming~~ ~~more~~ becoming more sucessful and enjoyed life.

The focus of your vision should be on developing and using your talents for the enjoyment and welfare of others as well as for your own benefit and that of your loved ones. If you make a lot of money by allowing your talents to flourish, that's great, but making a lot of money shouldn't be your goal. A successful life does not necessarily mean more money or a bigger house or vacations in Europe. A successful life can simply mean a life with meaning: a rewarding life; a life that contributes to the common good; a life that nurtures goodness in others.

That life will grow from your vision. But you need more than just a vision. You need a plan to make that vision a reality. And that's what we'll talk about in the next step.

Step 3: Develop Your Travel Plan

If you want to make good use of your time, you've got to know what's most important and then give it all you've got.

—Lee Iacocca

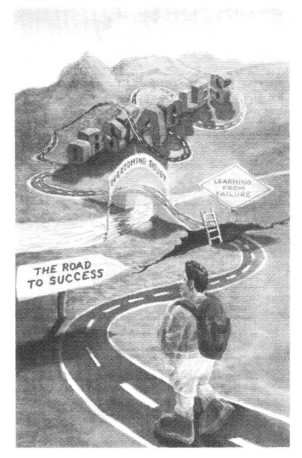

We are *all* gifted; we *all* have the potential to achieve great things. But all too many of us don't tap deeply into that potential because we give up when the road gets rocky. Anyone can stroll down a clear, smooth lane. But when the road takes twists and turns, when it becomes bumpy and dips and climbs, when you can't see too far into the distance because your focus is necessarily on the difficult steps immediately ahead of you, do you keep on keeping on, or do you stop and look for the nearest exit?

No one's road to success is easy. On the road to success, the two sure things are *failure* and *doubt.* You have to learn from the one and conquer the other to achieve success. And to do so, you need to have a travel plan in mind for that bumpy road. The plan has to be well developed, grounded in your values, and coming from your vision for yourself.

Creating visions, developing travel plans to achieve those visions, and experiencing success doesn't just happen to adults. It happens to young people in every venue: academics, art, music, writing, sports, achievement clubs, you name it. Don't think only in terms of your *future* success. Think in terms of success *now.* You'd be amazed at what you can make happen when you set your mind to it. But it doesn't just happen because you *want* it to happen. It happens because you *plan* to make it happen.

That's what this step is all about: planning to make it happen. In this step we'll help you turn your vision into reality by:

- Choosing action steps toward your goals
- Making time for goals and for all aspects of life
- Getting and keeping on schedule
- Staying focused on what's truly important

> On the road to success, the two sure things are *failure* and *doubt.* You have to learn from the one and conquer the other to achieve success.

Taking One Step at a Time

Whether you're a wrestler planning to win a league title next season or a student with an entrepreneurial bent who wants to start your own business and build a successful career, you need to plan the right steps. What's important at the moment is not how much you achieve, but how much you learn about the process for achieving. That's because once you learn the process, you can apply it in the field or area of your choice, anywhere you want to use the gifts you have.

> Don't plan for overnight success—plan for long-term success.

Each of us has limited time, energy, and resources, so it is not possible to do everything that might move us toward our goals. Deciding which steps to take can be difficult, but if you weigh your choices carefully, you can make great strides with just a few efficient steps rather than running all over the place trying to do too much. Effective planning involves prioritizing those steps that move you most efficiently toward your goal.

When you begin to actually work toward your goals through a plan of action, you assert power over your life. You prove that you have control. When you live life with purpose and energy by acting upon goals that are based in principles that you believe in, then you are living on your full power. You are fully engaged in life. You know who you are, where you are going, and what sort of person you want to be when you get there.

How do you develop a plan? Step by step. One foot in front of the other. Following the route that best serves your purposes, whether it is along a well-traveled highway over the river and through the woods, or along untraveled terrain. Carefully selecting the route that is right for you is critical: you don't rush the planning stage of your life's journey any

55

W hen you live life with purpose and energy by acting upon goals that are based in principles that you believe in, then you are living on your full power. You are fully engaged in life.

more than you would take off on a long trip without first studying the map to determine the best route to get where you want to go.

■ Action Steps Toward Your Goals

Let's consider the ten goals you listed on page 48 in step 2. Choose one of those ten goals. Write it here:

Save enough money for a car.

Now write down ten actions that will help you reach your goal. Don't worry about putting them in chronological order or in order of importance; just list ten steps. If you need help, ask a friend, a teacher, or one of your family members to help you brainstorm about actions you might take to move toward your goals.

1. *Get a job*
2. *Open a saving account*
3. *Search for insurance laws*
4. *Save money*
5. *Find the right first car*
6. *Get a credit score*
7. *Get a loan if needed*
8. *talk to a dealer*
9. *negotiate price*
10. *buy a car*

Now, identify the three of these ten actions that are most likely to help you achieve your goal. Write the three actions and rank them in order of most important to least important.

1. *get a job*
2. *look for a good car*
3. *save money*

You now have identified three important steps to take in reaching your goal. And you have begun to learn the process of developing a travel plan.

Getting—and Keeping—on Track

Determining what actions will help you best pursue your goals is only the first step in enacting your plan. The second step is devising a schedule for those actions. Time-management experts generally agree that the best thing to do is set up a weekly schedule. Scheduling, they say, is the bridge between knowing what to do and doing it.

Time management is a major issue for teens and adults alike. Four common causes of poor time management are the following:

- **Procrastination:** The first cause of poor time management is procrastination. You operate under the mistaken belief that you will have time later to do a task, and you never get to it.
- **Trying to do too much:** Another cause of poor time management is being unrealistic about how much you can get done, so you always bite off more than you can chew.
- **"Creeping":** A third cause is called task creeping. Before you are able to complete a task, you agree to take on another one. This happens again and again until you are overloaded and can't tend effectively to anything you have taken on.
- **"Jumping":** Related to task creeping is jumping from one task to another, either from lack of concentration, inability to prioritize tasks, or impending deadlines. The result is you are not able to complete any of the tasks very satisfactorily.

You need to be realistic about taking on new tasks or projects and about how much time you have to give to them, and you have to be wise in scheduling your time to accomplish your goals for tasks or projects not only effectively, but in a timely manner. Wasting time, or putting things off, or jumping from one thing to another won't get it done. You need to be a wise scheduler of your time.

▪ Time to Plan

How effective are you at planning your time? Complete this worksheet, total your points, and then see the scale at the end.

How often do you plan your day or your week in advance?

Never	(5 points)
Seldom	(4 points)
Sometimes	(3 points)
Frequently	(2 points)
Always	(1 point)

How often do you procrastinate on tasks you know you need to get done?

Never	(1)
Seldom	(2)
Sometimes	(3)
Frequently	(4)
Always	(5)

How often do you feel that you just don't have enough time to accomplish a task?

Never	(1)
Seldom	(2)

Sometimes   (3)
Frequently   (4)
Always   (5)

How often do you waste time in unproductive conversations and activities?
Never   (1)
Seldom   (2)
Sometimes   (3)
Frequently   (4)
Always   (5)

To what extent does your schedule allow time for the unexpected?
Never   (5)
Seldom   (4)
Sometimes   (3)
Frequently   (2)
Always   (1)

How often do you agree to take on another task before completing a task you are already working on?
Never   (1)
Seldom   (2)
Sometimes   (3)
Frequently   (4)
Always   (5)

How often do you find yourself rushing through tasks for various projects and completing none of them to your satisfaction because you don't have time to do so?
Never   (1)
Seldom   (2)
Sometimes   (3)
Frequently   (4)
Always   (5)

How often do you jump from task to task because you're not sure how to prioritize them?
Never   (1)
Seldom   (2)
Sometimes   (3)
Frequently   (4)
Always   (5)

How often do you lose a good idea because you were busy doing something else and didn't have time to write it down?

Never   (1)
Seldom   (2)
Sometimes   (3)
Frequently   (4)
Always   (5)

How often do you find yourself saying yes to a task or project when your schedule is already filled, but you want to be involved in the new task or project?

Never   (1)
Seldom   (2)
Sometimes   (3)
Frequently   (4)
Always   (5)

Score:

10 to 15	Excellent
16 to 20	Very good
21 to 25	Good
26 to 30	OK
31 to 50	Poor

How did you score? If you didn't score so well, pay special attention to the next section on how to improve your time management skills.

Two-Day Timesheet

Part of planning well is knowing how to use your time wisely. Do you really know how you spend your time? You will once you complete this next activity.

Keep an accurate two-day record of how you spend your time using the following chart to log your activities. Record each new activity and the time you spend on it. For example, if you study geometry for one hour, then talk on the phone for a half hour and then study social studies for two hours, your log should look like this:

- Study geometry   1 hour
- Talk on phone   .5 hour
- Study social studies   2 hours

It should not look like this:

- Study   3.5 hours

Also, don't clump all your classes together as "school"—log individual hours and classes!

▓ **Two-Day Timesheet**

Date	Time of Day	Activity	Time Spent
	Morning	Get ready for school	1 hour
		I.E + A.R	1 hour
		English	48 min
		Gym/health	48 min
		EBD	48 min
		Lunch	30 min
		S.S	48 min
	Afternoon	Science	46 min
		Geometry	48 min
		French	48 min
		Future city	2.5 hours
	Evening	H.W.	45 min
		Dinner	30 min
		E.D. time	1 hr.
		Shower	10 min
		Get ready for bed	30 min
		Go to bed	5 min

_____

_____

_____

_____

_____

▦ Making Time to Take Action

In the worksheet entitled "Action Steps Toward Your Goals" (page 56), you identified the three actions that would most help you achieve a particular goal. Review those three actions that you wrote down, and write them again in the space below.

Action 1 <u>Get a job</u>

Action 2 <u>look for a good per</u>

Action 3 <u>Save money</u>

Now, schedule those actions for a specific time on a specific day next week.

I will complete these activities at the following times:

Action 1: Day of week/Date <u>Sat / Sun</u> Time <u>12 hrs.</u>

Action 2: Day of week/Date <u>Every day</u> Time <u>5-10 min</u>

Action 3: Day of week/Date <u>Every day</u> Time <u>All day</u>

Now there's only one thing left to do: take action!

Staying Focused on Your Vision

You've probably seen photographs of carriage horses in New York's Central Park, along Michigan Avenue in Chicago, or in other cities around the world. Many of them wear blinders that allow them to see only where they are supposed to be going. The blinders block out distractions so that they keep on going in the right direction. That's what you need to do in pursuing your dreams and your vision. There are four keys to remember when you set out to pursue your vision for your life:

1. Knowing what *not* to do is just as important as knowing what to do
2. Don't allow the "urgent" things that cry out to you to distract you from the truly important things in your journey
3. Don't procrastinate
4. Do something that is truly important in moving you toward your goals every day

Knowing What *Not* to Do

Knowing what not to do is just as important as knowing what to do. Don't back down when faced with challenges or hard times as you follow your vision, but don't waste time on things you cannot control or that don't move you closer to your goals. For some of us, this may mean making wiser decisions about how to spend time and with whom we spend it. For others, it may mean letting go of things that bother us but that we can't change. Focus on the things that can be changed and actions that you can take in order to achieve your goals.

Problems outside your control are often related to something that has happened in the past. You can only influence your current and future behavior, so you should not waste your time worrying about something that is in the past. This is reflected in the Serenity Prayer: "Lord, grant me the power to accept the things that I cannot change, the courage to change the things I can, and the wisdom to know the difference."

Keeping Your Priorities Straight

Don't allow the "urgent" things that cry out to you to distract you from the truly important things in your journey. For example, it might be *important* that you get your American lit paper done within a few days, so you have to put off the *urgent* things like socializing with your friends or talking over serious matters with your girlfriend or boyfriend.

When you take charge of your time, you take charge of your life. How you spend your time reflects your priorities.

Have you ever had the experience of looking back and wondering why you paid attention to certain "urgent" things in your life when you should have been tending to things that were truly more important? As they say, hindsight is 20/20. The irony is that the urgent things in your life tug at your sleeves, shout, stamp their feet, whistle, do anything to get your attention, while the truly important things are in the background, waiting for you to come to them. They aren't going anywhere, but they often aren't in your face like urgent matters tend to be. So, it's easy to overlook the important things.

Taking Action *Now*

Don't procrastinate. Procrastination comes from fear. It's like a protective fence for those who want to stay within their comfort zone. *If I don't do anything,* think procrastinators, *no one will see my weaknesses or limitations. If I don't take part or take action, no one can judge me.* Procrastinators aren't people who don't know what to do; they're people who do know what to do, but for various reasons don't take action. This attitude makes it extremely hard to reach goals.

By not acting when you know you should be doing something, you waste time. Procrastinate too much and life will pass you by—you will feel stuck. If you keep putting off looking into colleges, if you keep wondering how you would fare in a sport or a club or on a committee, if you keep putting off your studies to watch TV or talk with your friends, then remember this: just like the person who sets his or her alarm, then shuts it off and oversleeps, *you snooze, you lose.*

Moving Toward Goals Daily

Do something that is truly important in moving you toward your goals every day. Invest your time in the important steps. When you take charge of your time, you take charge of your life. How you spend your time reflects your priorities. When you have trouble taking the steps to reach a goal, you need to ask yourself whether the goal really reflects your deepest needs, desires, and values—your true priorities in life. When goals come from your deepest needs and values, it's not hard to go after them.

▪ Four Keys to Staying Focused

You just read about four keys to staying focused on your vision. Complete this worksheet to see how well you're tuned in to your dreams and vision. Score yourself and see the scale at the end.

How often do you waste time on things you can't control?

Never	(1 point)
Seldom	(2 points)
Sometimes	(3 points)
Frequently	(4 points)
Always	(5 points)

How well are you able to let go of the past and focus on the present?

Extremely poorly	(5)
Not very well	(4)

OK   (3)
Very well   (2)
Extremely well (1)

How often are you distracted from truly important things by urgent things?

Never   (1)
Seldom   (2)
Sometimes (3)
Frequently (4)
Always   (5)

How often do you wish you could prioritize things better?

Never   (1)
Seldom   (2)
Sometimes (3)
Frequently (4)
Always   (5)

How often do you feel that your decisions are based on your needs, beliefs, and values?

Never   (5)
Seldom   (4)
Sometimes (3)
Frequently (2)
Always   (1)

How often do you procrastinate on important tasks, decisions, or issues?

Never   (1)
Seldom   (2)
Sometimes (3)
Frequently (4)
Always   (5)

How often do you act—or not act—out of fear, only to wish later that you had acted differently?

Never   (1)
Seldom   (2)
Sometimes (3)
Frequently (4)
Always   (5)

How often do you take actions or steps toward your goals?

Never   (5)
Seldom   (4)

Sometimes	(3)
Frequently	(2)
Always	(1)

How much of your time is spent according to your priorities and pursuing what you want to achieve?

None of my time	(5)
Little of my time	(4)
Some of my time	(3)
Most of my time	(2)
All of my time	(1)

How well do you take charge of your time on a day-to-day basis?

Extremely poorly	(5)
Not very well	(4)
OK	(3)
Very well	(2)
Extremely well	(1)

Score:

10 to 15	Excellent
16 to 20	Very good
21 to 25	Good
26 to 30	Okay
31 to 50	Poor

How did you score? If you didn't score so well, review and focus on those four keys to holding on to your dreams and vision.

Weekly Schedule

Part of knowing where you're going is making specific weekly plans. This activity will help you set up such a schedule.

You've listed goals and plans to reach those goals—now fill out the following weekly schedule to help you plan to actively work toward reaching those goals. This schedule should reflect not only your action plans for your goals; it should relate directly to your Success Circles and the Vision Statement that you created.

Be specific and realistic with the schedule. After the week is over, evaluate how well you stuck to your plan and how well you scheduled your week.

▪ Weekly Schedule

Monday

Time	Activities
6 A.M.	_____
7 A.M.	_____
8 A.M.	_____
9 A.M.	_____
10 A.M.	_____
11 A.M.	_____
12 NOON	_____
1 P.M.	_____
2 P.M.	_____
3 P.M.	_____
4 P.M.	_____
5 P.M.	_____
6 P.M.	_____
7 P.M.	_____
8 P.M.	_____
9 P.M.	_____

Tuesday

Time	Activities
6 A.M.	_____
7 A.M.	_____
8 A.M.	_____
9 A.M.	_____
10 A.M.	_____

11 A.M. _____

12 NOON _____

1 P.M. _____

2 P.M. _____

3 P.M. _____

4 P.M. _____

5 P.M. _____

6 P.M. _____

7 P.M. _____

8 P.M. _____

9 P.M. _____

Wednesday

Time   **Activities**

6 A.M. _____

7 A.M. _____

8 A.M. _____

9 A.M. _____

10 A.M. _____

11 A.M. _____

12 NOON _____

1 P.M. _____

2 P.M. _____

3 P.M. _____

4 P.M. _____

5 P.M. _____

6 P.M. _____

7 P.M. _____

8 P.M. _____

9 P.M. _____

Thursday

Time   **Activities**

6 A.M. _____

7 A.M. _____

8 A.M. _____

9 A.M. _____

10 A.M. _____

11 A.M. _____

12 NOON _____

1 P.M. _____

2 P.M. _____

3 P.M. _____

4 P.M. _____

5 P.M. _____

6 P.M. _____

7 P.M. _____

8 P.M. _____

9 P.M. _____

Friday

Time   **Activities**

6 A.M. _____

7 A.M. _____

8 A.M. _____

9 A.M. _____

10 A.M. _____

11 A.M. _____

12 NOON _____

1 P.M. _____

2 P.M. _____

3 P.M. _____

4 P.M. _____

5 P.M. _____

6 P.M. _____

7 P.M. _____

8 P.M. _____

9 P.M. _____

Saturday

Time   **Activities**

6 A.M. _____

7 A.M. _____

8 A.M. _____

9 A.M. _____

10 A.M. _____

11 A.M. _____

12 NOON _____

1 P.M. _____

2 P.M. _____

3 P.M. _____

4 P.M. _____

5 P.M. _____

6 P.M. _____

7 P.M. _____

8 P.M. _____

9 P.M. _____

Sunday

Time   **Activities**

6 A.M. _____

7 A.M. _____

8 A.M. _____

9 A.M. _____

10 A.M. _____

11 A.M. _____

12 NOON _____

1 P.M. _____

2 P.M. _____

3 P.M. _____

4 P.M. _____

5 P.M. _____

6 P.M. _____

7 P.M. _____

8 P.M. _____

9 P.M. _____

Making Final Travel Plans

Once you have a plan for your journey complete with routes to specific stops along the way to your ultimate destination mapped out, it is important to check to see if you are packed properly. Are you fully prepared to begin the Success Process? Having a vision and goals and a plan to reach them is essential, but you also have to make sure that you are properly prepared to begin your journey and to undertake it in a manner that is consistent with the principles and beliefs that you have chosen to guide your life.

When you are taking actions to reach your goals, always keep an eye on what is most important to you, so that in the process of going after your goals you don't get off track as a person. We all have heard of people who have achieved fame and fortune, only to have everything fall apart because they neglected other important aspects of their lives.

What if you achieved your goal to become a doctor, only to discover that you'd neglected your health so badly that you could no longer continue working? What if you fulfilled your vision of getting your master's degree, but had no one to share the victory with because in your march to that goal you neglected your relationships with friends and family? In the next step, you will learn some rules of the road, designed to help you stay on track and in touch with what is important in life as you journey through the Success Process.

Step 4: Master the Rules of the Road

Values are guiding devices to enhance our ability to achieve our purposes.

—Allan Cox

The nine-step process in which you are engaged has, so far, enabled you to develop a better idea of who you are, create a vision of where you want your life to go, and develop goals designed to help attain your vision. You also have Success Circles, which contain what is most important to you and which will help you focus your efforts as you mature and adjust your vision, dreams, and goals. In the last step, you worked on developing a plan that will help you focus on your vision.

Now you're ready to go, right? Wrong. The road to success is a rocky one. Having a plan to negotiate that road is crucial, but there's a second part to being prepared for that rocky road: you need to have some tools handy to help you when things break down on the road—or to help *prevent* breakdowns. Those tools include determination, conscience, willpower, imagination, and balance. You also need to have some rules of the road to guide you along the way.

Five tools and a set of rules: that's what you need to keep you going when the road gets rough and you appear to be going off course. We'll start with the tools first.

Determination

Can you imagine anyone who is truly successful—and successful for the long run—who is not determined? You have to not only plan for success; you have to *make it happen*. That comes from determination. Every time you fail, try again. You have to keep on keeping on when you are pursuing your dreams and goals. It is *always* too early to quit. That is an unspoken motto for all successful people. If you set goals and make plans, you are on the right path, but if you aren't devoted to them, if you give up when the going gets tough or if you fall apart in the face of obstacles or opposition, you'll get nowhere.

▪ "Don't Tell Me I Can't Do It"

For some people, words telling them that they can't do something are like premium-grade fuel for their engines—it's just what they need to get going. For others, hearing negative messages or facing obstacles makes them veer from their chosen path, even if that path is the right one for them. Answer the following ten True-False questions to see how you rate in your determination.

When people tell me I'm not capable of accomplishing something that is very important to me, I generally believe them and give up, or I alter my goals and shoot for something less than I really want.

True   False

When I come upon a roadblock and I don't know how to get around it on my own, I generally don't ask for outside help from friends, parents, teachers, or mentors. I try to figure it out on my own or just give up.

True   False

When people doubt that I can do something so much that it feels like an attack on my self-worth, I stop focusing on my goal and spend my time trying to defend myself from the attack.

True   False

I would rather be well-*liked* than well-*respected*. I'd prefer, of course, to be both liked and respected, but if I could only choose one, I'd choose to be liked.

    True   False

If the goals that come from my deepest values are not in line with those of my friends and peers, then I will change or drop those goals rather than lose my friends.

    True   False

In order not to hurt or upset my friends, I will compromise my deepest-held values and goals.

    True   False

In the face of adversity, I stand strong for my beliefs and values—unless I feel that the consequences—such as ridicule, loss of friends, disapproval from parents or teachers or coaches, or the like—are too great.

    True   False

Even when I believe strongly in something, I am often unable to overcome adversity because I am afraid of failing. Rather than risk failure, I would choose not to try to overcome adversity.

    True   False

Roadblocks are signs that I am on the wrong road. People who are truly successful understand this and learn to go with the flow and get on a different road.

    True   False

When I come upon a roadblock, my first thought is to drop or change my plans, especially if the roadblock challenges me in new ways and forces me to step out of my comfort zone.

    True   False

Scale:

> 0-3 "false" answers—you are not very determined
> 4–6 "false" answers—you are sometimes determined, but are often held back by adversity
> 7–8 "false" answers—you are usually quite determined, but certain situations tend to hold you back
> 9–10 "false" answers—you are extremely determined!

Don't be too upset if you scored low. You can develop determination as you grow. Life presents us with constant challenges through which we can grow and stretch our abilities to use determination to help us achieve our goals.

Now answer the following questions related to determination.

An example from my own life that best illustrates my determination to succeed in the face of adversity or obstacles is:

_____

_____

_____

_____

_____

_____

We all have gone through situations where, in hindsight, we wish we had stuck with our deeper values but were somehow swayed from doing so. Detail one time when you wish you had stuck to your guns but were swayed by friends or other influences to do something you didn't believe was right or that made you abandon or change a goal:

_____

_____

_____

_____

_____

In retrospect, what could you have done differently in that situation? How could stronger determination have helped you?

_____

_____

_____

_____

_____

If you had done things differently, as you've just described, how might the outcome have been different?

_____

_____

_____

_____

What feelings come to mind when you think of determined people? Awe? Respect? Inspiration?

_____

_____

_____

_____

What is one area in your life right now that could benefit from you being more determined?

_____

_____

_____

_____

What steps can you take to be more determined in that area?

_____

_____

_____

_____

Conscience

Your conscience is the inner voice that serves as a quality-control check on your actions. Your conscience says, _Is this what I should be doing? Why am I doing this?_ It monitors your actions and attempts to keep them in line with your belief system.

Your conscience is there to guide you—if you allow it to—in everyday circumstances: whether or not to cheat on a test, or to gossip and belittle people behind their backs, or to use tobacco, alcohol, or other drugs. Oftentimes the things you are tempted to do or like to do are things that keep you from achieving goals and making your vision be-

77

come reality. People who don't listen very well to their consciences are the types who later say, "I should have done such-and-such" or "I didn't think my doing such-and-such would result in *this.*"

Let your conscience be your guide so that you aren't deterred from your path. Your conscience is one of the most useful tools you can use to keep you on target to reach your goals.

Willpower

Your *will* gives you the power to follow your conscience rather than outside influences and distractions. You might feel compelled to talk about someone behind his or her back or to buy something you can't afford, but your conscience sounds the alert and your will gives you the power to choose what is most compatible with your belief system and circumstances.

Your will, then, helps you overcome your moods and fleeting desires to keep you on track for a life of integrity. You *can* say no to tobacco, alcohol, and other drugs. You *can* say no to gossiping and talking about others behind their backs. You *can* say no to taking part in activities that you know are wrong or that keep you from pursuing your goals. Your will keeps you going when the going gets tough, because it holds you to your long-term vision, blocking out short-term distractions.

"Jessica never does what she says she will do. Why believe her?" "Antoine will come through if it's easy enough. But if things get tough, then forget it. You never know about him." These kids are being branded—they are developing reputations for not coming through. It is becoming their *brand name*—what they are known for. How you use your willpower will have a direct effect on what your brand name becomes.

Think about it. Coca-Cola has a brand. You expect a certain quality of taste with every can or bottle of Coke. Tide has a brand. You expect your laundry to come out fresh and clean every time you use Tide. You count on these products; they are known for their consistency and quality. That happens with people, too. You develop your own brand name for yourself. It's up to you how good a brand that is.

■ Build Your Own Life Brand!

So what is a brand? A brand is a promise. Over time, strong brands inspire trust by constantly keeping their promise. Strong brands offer consistent long-term performance. Strong brands demonstrate a commitment to quality.

If you have any goals or dreams for your life, then, whether you realize it or not, you are already pitching your own brand every day in many different ways—whether you are a high school student hoping to make the grade for college or an athlete competing for a position on a team. Each and every day, you communicate who you are and what you stand for. This is your promise, your image, your brand.

Describe the image you would like to project of yourself—your "Life Brand." Start by identifying the qualities or characteristics that distinguish you from others. These are your brand assets. For example, Do you show up on time, every time? Are you a good listener or an effective communicator? Are you trustworthy? Loyal? Do you have strong leadership skills? Are you creative or good at solving problems? Record your Life Brand below.

_____

_____

_____

_____

_____

_____

_____

Imagination

Conscience is a rudder to guide you through choppy waters. Willpower is the inner strength to help you stay the course. *Imagination* is your ability to be creative in finding ways to either steer clear of those choppy waters or steer safely through them. People who tap into their imagination find solutions where others only see problems. Willpower is used largely to say no to various situations; imagination is used to say yes to various solutions that will help you achieve your goals.

> The best way to determine your own destiny is to create it and control it. This is a part of what true freedom is all about.

Imagination is directly connected to vision. The greater your ability to imagine, the greater your ability to create a large and meaningful vision for yourself. People who use their imagination will tend to think "outside the box." They see things in different ways; they look at problems from various angles and perspectives, and they aren't afraid to dream, to speculate, and to suggest alternatives. When you use your imagination, you greatly improve your chances to succeed, because you open up so many opportunities for yourself.

By using your imagination, you can learn to see yourself responding to problems, challenges, and bad situations in a more positive and productive manner. And you can use your will to choose the best response over one driven by your emotions or moods. The best

way to determine your own destiny is to create it and control it. This is a part of what true freedom is all about.

■ Conscience, Willpower, and Imagination: Three Powerful Tools for the Road

Starting off on your road to success not equipped with these three tools is asking for trouble. Complete this worksheet to begin developing these tools for your journey.

You can use your conscience as a rudder to help guide you in making difficult decisions. How well do you usually listen to your conscience and use it in making tough decisions?

- Not well at all
- I use it sometimes
- I use it quite often in making tough decisions

In what types of decisions or situations do you find yourself most likely to act against your conscience?

_____

_____

_____

When you act against your conscience, what is a common outcome?

_____

_____

_____

What price do you pay for acting against your conscience?

_____

_____

_____

Describe a situation when you were tempted to act against your conscience but instead listened to your conscience and were glad you did.

_____

_____

_____

Having a conscience would be quite frustrating if we didn't have the willpower to *act* on what it tells us. What are the areas or situations in your life that call on your strongest willpower?

_____

_____

_____

Why do you need strong willpower in these areas or situations?

_____

_____

_____

Describe a situation in which you surprised yourself by acting on your conscience when you didn't think you had the willpower to do so.

_____

_____

_____

If you could have the willpower to change one of your attitudes or habits, what would you change?

_____

_____

You can use imagination as a bridge across dangerous waters. Describe a time when you used your imagination to see an escape route or path that no one else around you saw.

_____

_____

_____

▦ Terms Clarification Sheet

In this activity you'll define terms that can act as guideposts along your journey through life. Definitions should not overlap—no two words should have exactly the same definition. No dictionaries allowed!

- Self-discipline: _____

_____

- Trustworthiness: _____

_____

- Integrity: _____

_____

- Conscience: _____

_____

- Willpower: _____

_____

- Determination: _____

_____

- Sincerity: _____

_____

- Honesty: _____

_____

Balance

In developing your plan for acting on your goals, you need to understand that your physical, social, mental, and spiritual health are all connected. By tending to all of them, you can find a path to your goals that will keep you balanced, fulfilled, and happy on your journey. If you neglect any one of them you run the risk of falling off the path or going off in a direction that will not be as good for you. Let's take a brief look at each aspect of health.

Physical Health

Your physical well-being is vital in your pursuit of a better life. Take care of your body by exercising, eating well, and getting adequate rest. If you don't do those things, you might hide poor physical health for a while, but eventually it will deteriorate and affect all parts of your life.

It is hard to concentrate on tasks when you're in poor physical health. Relationships can suffer, and focusing on spiritual growth can be a challenge. When you work out every day, you build energy and a sense of empowerment. Being physically healthy adds a great deal to every other aspect of your life.

Social Health

Your social well-being revolves around your relationships. There is no substitute for real social interaction; all people need it. Nor is there any substitute for the qualities it takes to build relationships. You can fake charm, you can smile and be a smooth talker, but eventually you have to prove your integrity, your trustworthiness, and your sincerity. To live without love, trust, and mutual support is to live a hollow life. If you feel that your social health is not what it should be, take a step back and consider how others view you. Are you trustworthy? Do you keep your word? Are you a good friend, someone who will *listen* as well as talk? Are you open with others? Are you a *giver* as well as a *taker* in relationships? Are you always talking about your own needs, wanting others to focus on those needs, but never willing to focus on others' needs?

Mental Health

You fuel your mental well-being by being positive and optimistic. You maintain it through continual learning and growth. Obviously, you cannot pursue a better life without being in good mental health with an alert mind. For a time, it was considered a cliché to urge people to be optimistic in their mental approach, but that has changed.

83

Increasingly, researchers are finding that an optimistic attitude is every bit as important as a high IQ in predicting an individual's ability to achieve his or her goals and dreams.

These researchers have found that people with a pessimistic approach to life tend to believe that bad things are inevitable, that they somehow triggered them, and that the problem will last a long time, undermining all of their plans. This negative attitude feeds on itself and fosters depression. Pessimists focus on the problems that they feel are facing them.

A person with an optimistic mental attitude, on the other hand, tends to view bad times as temporary, failure as a step to eventual success, and misfortune as the result of circumstances beyond his or her control. Optimists focus on solutions that they feel await their discovery.

Spiritual Health

Your spiritual well-being begins with how you feel about yourself, but it does not end there. It runs much deeper into the realm of how you relate to others, respond to others, and what you bring into the lives of others. Having a solid spiritual base promotes self-discipline, an inner calm, and an ability to love others as much as you love yourself—all of which are essential tools for your journey to a better life.

Understand, though, that your life has a spiritual quality only when it is based on something other than self. Animals live for themselves. Humans, we hope, live to serve something greater than the individual. Organized religion is a primary method to build spiritual health, but there are many other ways, including the study of ancient philosophies. Some people build spiritual health by reading Scripture, some by meditating in a darkened room, some by sitting on the beach basking in nature's beauty, some by listening to beautiful music, reading powerful literature, or looking at great works of art.

There are those who act as though this aspect of human existence has no meaning to their lives. True, it *is* possible to achieve your goals without having a healthy spiritual life. Whether or not you can fully appreciate and enjoy those successes without a spiritual base, however, is another matter.

▧ Leading a Balanced, Healthy Life

The road to success is best traveled when the physical, social, mental, and spiritual aspects of your life are all healthy and in balance with one another. Complete this worksheet on those four aspects to see how balanced your life is.

What do you do now to lead a healthy physical life?

_____

_____

What steps could you take to improve your physical health?

_____

_____

_____

What do you do now to lead a healthy social life?

_____

_____

_____

What steps could you take to improve your social health?

_____

_____

_____

What do you do now to lead a healthy mental life?

_____

_____

_____

What steps could you take to improve your mental health?

_____

_____

_____

What do you do now to lead a healthy spiritual life?

_____

_____

_____

What steps could you take to improve your spiritual health?

_____

_____

_____

Rules of the Road

If the *tools* for the road are determination, conscience, willpower, imagination, and balance, then what are the *rules* of the road? They are the values and principles that you have chosen to guide your life. They should help you stay on course toward your goals and give you the strength and determination to fight and overcome distractions, hardships, and obstacles.

Here are five rules of the road:

1. **Be honest.** You have no value to other people if they cannot believe what you say. Trust is built on perceptions of honesty. If you are honest with people even when you fail, you at least maintain credibility over time.

2. **Do the work that is required.** What you put into any project or plan is reflected in how it turns out. Why waste your time doing something half-heartedly? You know in your heart what you need to do to realize your goals. If you do less, it only hurts you. Don't make excuses—do the work required.

3. **Maintain a positive attitude.** Being positive begins with eliminating the negative. That includes negative thoughts in your mind, negative relationships, anything that interferes with your ability to move forward.

4. **Take the time to think things through.** We have a wonderful capacity to think, but too often, we submit to the temptation to act without giving enough thought beforehand. Much of what we do is reaction, because immediate action gives more instant gratification, but if you think about what you are doing first, you eliminate many errors and crises. Those who take the time to think and plan out their lives are the ones who get the greatest benefit out of whatever they are involved in.

5. **Look at the big picture.** Too many people think first and foremost from a selfish perspective, from the point of "me." That is small-picture thinking. If you look at the big picture, your thought process revolves around how you can make a difference in the lives of others. Looking at the big picture also gives you perspective on how your actions and words will impact those around you. When you operate from this perspective, you offer leadership to those around you, and being a leader opens up greater opportunities for you.

In the next activity, you will develop your own rules of the road. Refer to these rules as you take action on your goals. Check them if you feel your life has lost balance. Keep in mind that while you are becoming goal-oriented; it is important not to lose sight of the things you value in life. (Recall the activity where you wrote the introduction to your autobiography.) Remember the key questions:

- What kind of person do you want to be at the end of your life's journey?
- What do you want your legacy to be to your family?
- What will people say about you when you are gone?

▪ Creating Your Own Rules of the Road

In the space below, write your own rules of the road to help guide the way you live. Write as many as you think are pertinent to you. Review them often so that you stay on track.

_____

_____

_____

_____

_____

_____

Fulfilling Responsibilities Along the Way

One last issue to consider before setting off on your journey: you cannot leave your responsibilities at home. It is vital that you consider how your actions along the way will affect all aspects of your life, every relationship and responsibility that you have or will have along the way.

Each of us has many roles to fill. I am an employer, a board member, a partner, a father, a son, a friend, and a club member, among other roles. When I put together a plan for achieving my goals, I had to consider how my actions would impact each of those roles and how I could balance them all while pursuing my vision.

In the next worksheet, you'll consider the roles you play and your long-term goals in the context of those roles so that you can fulfill your responsibilities while fulfilling your vision.

▪ Roles and Goals

Consider all of your relationships, affiliations, and duties and then write down the roles that you fill. For instance, you might be a student, a son, a friend, and a band member; a student, a daughter, a sister, a friend, and an athlete.

Role 1 _____

Role 2 _____

Role 3 _____

Role 4 _____

Role 5 _____

Do you neglect some roles because you dwell too much on the others? Which of your roles seems most neglected?

_____

Are all of your roles in harmony with your vision for your life? If not, should you consider eliminating some roles? (For instance, if you listed "boyfriend" or "girlfriend," but you feel that you are neglecting your role there, perhaps it's because your day is so filled in fulfilling your other roles that you don't have the time to give to the relationship what it deserves.)

_____

_____

_____

Review your roles and determine what is most important. List those roles again, and write down your long-term goal for each role.

EXAMPLE: In my role as a student, I will take the classes that will best prepare me for college. I will take classes in my areas of interest and take leadership roles in those classes, because I know the more I put into a class, the more I get out of it.

Role 1 _____

    Goal: _____

Role 2 _____

    Goal: _____

Role 3 _____

    Goal: _____

Role 4 _____

    Goal: _____

Role 5 _____

    Goal: _____

You have, or will have, many roles to fill. You will probably have roles that relate to family, education, sports, drama, studying, social relationships, and virtually every other aspect of your life. You will need to consider how much time to invest in each role and whether or not you neglect other roles by dwelling too much on any one of them. Weigh the importance of each role and whether or not each matches with your vision. Perhaps you will need to limit some roles. The bottom line is that you determine which aspects of your life are most important and then act accordingly. Your time and efforts devoted to each role should clearly reflect the relative importance of each role. Life is a process of continually creating balance while growing, achieving goals, creating new goals, accepting new challenges and responsibilities, and enjoying the experience of fashioning a successful and meaningful life.

At the beginning of this chapter I tried to slow down those of you who were ready to barge out the door and embark on your journey without having the five tools to use along the way, without having any rules of the road to use as guideposts. Now that we've discussed the tools and rules, we're ready to embark. The next chapter, however, addresses those who would prefer to stay at home, to stay in their comfort zones. There, we'll talk about stepping outside the box, venturing into personally uncharted territory. Because creating and fulfilling a vision necessarily means going places you haven't gone before.

Step 5: Step into the Outer Limits

Fear is an illusion.

—Michael Jordan

You are now halfway through the Success Process and are approaching the point of being prepared and self-confident about embarking upon your journey in pursuit of a better life. So far, you have prepared for the journey by:

- Increasing your self-awareness so that you better understand your emotions and feelings
- Creating a vision of your dreams and goals
- Devising a plan to pursue those goals
- Developing your own rules of the road to help you stay focused and to keep you from losing sight of the people and principles that are important to you

As you proceed on your journey in pursuit of a better life, you may begin to feel uncomfortable because you are entering new and unfamiliar territory. Pursuing your dreams forces you to leave your established comfort zone and move into areas where you may feel uncomfortable and as though you do not have as much control as you once had.

Loss of control is a scary thing for most people—no one likes the thought of losing control, even when, in truth, he or she may not really be in control in the first place. It is natural for people to want to stay with what is familiar and comfortable in their lives rather than for them to venture into the unknown. Most people want to stay within their comfort zones, where they feel safe and secure.

> **P**ush yourself to your own outer limits in becoming all you are destined to become.

Fear of the unknown is one of the greatest obstacles that you will face in life. But if you want a better life, you must learn to overcome that natural fear and step outside what has become comfortable and familiar. You must risk losing control in order to push yourself into the outer limits of your abilities and talents. That is how you move to a higher level of achievement. It is the way to a better life.

Do not compromise your goals, dreams, or guiding principles and values. Push yourself to your own outer limits in becoming all you are destined to become.

Extending Your Limits

You have numerous opportunities to extend yourself, go where you've never gone before, and grow through the experience of testing your limits. One way to look at it is to consider your life as a circle with opportunities for growth all around its outer border. There is no single door through which you must walk to push through to the "other side"; you can stretch yourself and grow—in effect, go outside your circle—from anyplace within. All around that circle you could label the things that are important to you—family, friends, education, personal development, specific goals and aspirations, and so on. And in each area you could take steps beyond the familiar, into uncharted territory and new growth. People who are successful are forever expanding their circles. This is a lifelong process.

If you want to be successful in this process, you must be willing to do two things: leave your comfort zone and use all your talent.

Leaving Your Comfort Zone

When your comfort zone isn't even truly comfortable but you stay in it because you would rather deal with the known than the unknown, your life is being guided by fear, not hope. That is no way to live. In fact, you are not really living when your fears control your actions. Instead, you are hiding from life.

As you proceed on your journey in pursuit of a better life, you may begin to feel uncomfortable because you are entering new territory. Pursuing your dreams, however, requires you to leave your comfort zone and to push into areas where you at first have less control. When you set out on your journey, though, you have to be willing to grow, to push your talents to the outer limits. That means pushing beyond what is known to you, taking risks, and learning to view failure as merely a step, rather than a defeat, in your journey along the Success Process.

We all have our comfort zones. They aren't, in and of themselves, bad things—they simply are indicators of the areas of our lives in which we feel most safe and secure. The goal here, then, is not to go toward a life of feeling unsafe and insecure. Rather, it's to continually stretch those comfort zones—which necessarily means stepping outside them to experience the unknown—and to make the unknown known, to, in essence, feel more and more comfortable with bigger and better things.

Using *All* Your Talent

It's easy to get comfortable at one level of achievement and then just kick back and coast. But, then, before you know what hit you, you find yourself *stuck*. One morning you wake up, look around and ask yourself, "What happened to my dream for my life? What about all those great things I was going to accomplish? All the adventures and dreams I had envisioned for my life? How did I get stuck?"

You get stuck by forgetting that life is a process of continual striving and challenge, of pushing your talents and knowledge. Sounds like work, doesn't it? That's why so many people get stuck. And it's not just people undergoing so-called midlife crises that feel stuck. It's also young adults, not much older than yourself. It's people who work in dead-end jobs or who are in bad relationships. It's people who have no idea what they want out of life and then blame life or other people for their troubles. It's people who live down to their low expectations for themselves and who suffer in silence, not wanting to draw attention to themselves. It's people who make bad choices early on in life and then don't know how to choose something better.

What about you? Do you get up in the morning excited about the potential for the day? Do you have a vision for your future and are you taking steps to attain that vision? Or are you just coasting, no plan, no destination in mind, no clue as to what you can do today to build toward a better tomorrow, skirting every challenge that comes your way? At the end of your life, will you look back and say, "I used life up! I rode it all the way, I took all of my talents and abilities as far as they would go"? Or will you say, "I stopped too soon. I sold myself short. I could have done better, I could have done more. I settled for the consolation prize instead of the grand prize"?

Don't compromise your goals and dreams. When you live life to the fullest, you don't *settle* for anything—you use up all of your energy. And at the end, you check out of this world with all of your gauges on empty, every talent and ability and interest exhausted.

The Success Process is really an inner journey and it requires courage to take the risks along the way and to truly use all your talents as you go.

Extending Boundaries, Expending Talents

To live to your full potential, you will always face risks; growth requires you to leave your comfort zone. Leaving a comfort zone takes courage. This worksheet will help you explore your comfort zone, as well as ways to get the most out of your talents.

Consider one of the important areas of your life: education, personal development, relationships, or individual pursuits such as music, the arts, or sports. Consider an area in which you feel competent, yet somewhat stagnant, an area in which you haven't experienced too much growth in the last year or so. You have, in effect, established your "comfort zone" in it and haven't pushed beyond—even though you may be experiencing a certain level of success in it. But you feel, deep down, that you can do *more*. When you stop to really think about it, you get frustrated, because you're just doing the "same old same old." Now answer these questions:

What is your comfort zone? In the particular area of your life that you have chosen to examine here, what are you comfortable in doing or accomplishing?

_____

_____

_____

What potential action or growth in this area of your life makes you begin to feel *uncomfortable?*

_____

_____

_____

Why do you think that such growth or action makes you feel uncomfortable?

_____

_____

_____

What would you *really* like to achieve in this area?

_____

_____

_____

What holds you back from achieving this, and why does it (or why do these things) hold you back?

_____

_____

_____

If you took steps beyond your comfort zone, what might happen?

_____

_____

_____

> If you continue to do what you have always done, you will continue to get the same result you have always gotten. But if you take well-calculated risks, you can make great progress.

In step 2, "Create Your Vision," you explored your talents and ways you could envision using your talents. The goal is to not just know what your talents are, but to *use* them. Now take the time to dream a little dream—in fact, two dreams.

Dream 1: Describe an easy way to use your talents in a career after you're finished with your education and are making your own way in the world. This way is the most obvious way and while it would call on your talents, it wouldn't necessarily stretch you or help you use those talents to the fullest. This way involves little risk; the path is pretty clear and the outcome is pretty easy to predict.

_____

_____

_____

Dream 2: Now describe a way in which you might use your talents that would truly challenge you—a way that involves risk and that energizes you to meet the challenges you would face. This way would be exciting, perhaps sometimes unnerving, but ultimately many times more rewarding than the "easy way" described in Dream 1.

_____

_____

_____

Which dream do you want to follow? Why?

_____

_____

_____

Taking Risks

Just as a tree grows by pushing buds up through the existing branches, you have to push yourself to grow beyond your current circumstances. This is where you have to walk the walk if you are serious about changing your life. It takes courage to take risks, to do things that you feel may expose you to the possibility of danger, loss, or failure.

Because of those potentially negative outcomes, most people—outside of stuntmen and daredevils—avoid taking risks as much as possible. But can you really escape taking risks in life? What can you do that has no risk to it? Love your family? Coast through school, taking the easiest classes and not getting involved in clubs and extracurricular activities that are in your areas of interest? Go along with the crowd for fear of being singled out as different?

The truth is that nothing is risk-free. Loving your family members involves the risk of losing them or having them hurt you with their behavior, but no one would consider withholding love rather than taking that risk. Any relationship involves risk, but if you spend your whole life avoiding involvement because you don't want to get hurt, what sort of life will you have? A lonely one.

RISK-TAKERS...

1) Need courage and strength to take on fears.

2) Must believe in their ability to overcome obstacles and solve problems.

3) Must be willing to experience failure

95

Coasting through school and through life brings with it the risk of boredom and of dissatisfaction with life—or, rather, with your *response* to life. There are few things as draining and depressing as taking the safe and easy way out and knowing that in doing so you are merely coasting. Coasting may be easy, but it's far from exhilarating and fulfilling.

Going along with the crowd can be rife with risks, depending on the crowd you run with. It might be the easiest solution for the moment, but if you go with the flow and follow the crowd, you might be following them down a path that leads to trouble with your parents or the law, to getting low grades or getting kicked out of school and having limited job opportunities later in life, and so on. "The crowd" is *not* a good barometer for the risks you should take and the decisions you should make.

In reality, you are always taking risks; sometimes doing nothing about your situation is itself a risk. Risk is like a coin with two sides: on one side, there is the possibility of failure, on the other is the opportunity for gain. Remember this about risks: If you continue to do what you have always done, you will continue to get the same result you have always gotten. But if you take well-calculated risks, you can make great progress.

Focus, then, not on whether you should take risks, but on what risks you should take, how you should take them, and what attributes you need to be an effective risk-taker. Here are some of those attributes:

- To be a risk-taker, you need courage and mental and moral strength to take on your fears.

    Mental and moral strength comes from a clear vision of what you want for your life and from a focus on your deepest values, needs, and desires. Clear vision and strong focus give you the power to pursue your goals in spite of fears and challenges.

- As a risk taker, you must believe in your ability to overcome obstacles and to solve problems.

    A can-do attitude is essential for taking risks. When you have this attitude, you understand that failure is not the end of the road. You realize that through failure you can learn how to succeed and grow. The lessons you learn from things that don't work help you to discover those things that do work.

- As a risk-taker, you must be willing to experience failure.

    It is up to you to decide whether the failures you do encounter will become defeats or whether they will lead to successes. When you learn to take risks and to view failure as part of the Success Process, you establish a pattern of continual growth. By living in this manner, you are always expanding your experience base, building on your strengths, and fortifying your self-confidence. That is why it is so important to learn to view failure as merely a lesson learned, a helpful marker that gives you a grasp for what you can and cannot do *at that point* in your life.

◼ Your Risk-Taking Profile

How are you at taking risks? Answer the following questions to determine your willingness to take risks.

What is the one risk you could take today that would move you most efficiently and effectively toward fulfilling your vision of a better life?

_____

_____

_____

What is the one thing you fear the most about taking that risk?

_____

_____

_____

What one habit or thing holds you back from taking that risk?

_____

_____

_____

How would taking this risk change your life?

_____

_____

_____

Identify two risks you have taken during the last year.
Risk A:

_____

_____

Risk B:

_____

_____

Now, select one of those risks and answer the following questions about your decision to take that risk.

Your goal in taking this risk was . . .

_____

_____

Your backup plan if things did not work out was . . .

_____

_____

The people who supported you in taking this risk were . . .

_____

_____

Taking this risk resulted in . . .

_____

_____

Complete the following sentences regarding this risk.

I had the courage to face my fears in taking this risk because . . .

_____

_____

_____

I believed in my ability to overcome obstacles and solve problems in taking this risk because . . .

_____

_____

_____

I was willing to experience failure in this risk because . . .

_____

_____

_____

Now answer the questions about taking risks in general.

In matters that are important to me, I face my fears and take risks . . .

    Always   Usually   Sometimes   Once in a while   Never

I believe in my ability to overcome obstacles and solve problems in taking risks . . .

    Always   Usually   Sometimes   Once in a while   Never

I am willing to experience failure in taking risks . . .

    Always   Usually   Sometimes   Once in a while   Never

Looking Before You Leap

Taking risks is essential to living a fulfilling and successful life, but I'm not saying that you blindly enter into a risk on a whim. When you consider risk, you must also consider consequences, and you need to take on risks with confidence. Taking risks takes courage, belief in yourself, and a willingness to fail. It also takes wisdom and faith.

Taking a risk is like leaping over an obstacle or a chasm that separates you from what you want. If you are certain that the risk is worth it, you can make that leap with determination, enthusiasm, and focus. But if you aren't so sure, you won't be as determined, enthusiastic, or focused, and in all likelihood, you won't make it. Instead of taking opportunities as they appear, you will be torn by indecision and ambivalence. Should you run for student council or not? Should you go out for track or not? Should you try out for this play or not? Indecision can be dangerous. In every wildlife documentary I've ever seen, the predator always gets the one animal that can't decide which way to run. Indecision might not result in you being eaten up literally, of course, but it can so consume you that you can't act on your vision for yourself.

Now, you aren't an impala running from the lions, so you can take time to evaluate the risks you take. Make sure the risk is in line with your principles, values, and beliefs before you make the leap. Measure the costs versus the gains. The more valued the gain, the more willing you should be to risk the cost.

> Fears can haunt and control you when you lack faith in your ability to overcome them and the courage to take them on.

No matter the situation, you need to consider the potential good that can come out of taking the risk, how it might positively affect goals you have and the vision you have for your life, and weigh that against the costs involved. Some risks, as you evaluate them, may not be worth your time, but others—even if you see only a slim chance for immediate payback—may be worth taking, because you'll learn from the process even if it turns out to be a "failure."

Overcoming Fear

You might say, "I've calculated the risk involved and I really want to take it, because I really think it's worth it—but I'm still stuck." I'd respond that most likely you're stuck in fear.

You cannot live your life in fear of what might happen. You must live according to your vision for a better life. The greatest reason why people do not take risks is fear of the unknown. The greatest way to overcome fear is to face it.

To face fear, you need faith and courage. You have to have faith that there really is no bogeyman under the bed and the courage to look down there to confirm it. Fears can haunt and control you when you lack faith in your ability to overcome them and the courage to take them on. Fear defeats you when you allow it to condition your mind, to make you a coward.

We all have fears, but fears are real only when we make them so by investing too much in them. When we allow fear to dominate our lives, we give it too much power. Often, fear is the only thing that stands between us and our vision for a better life, and if we don't develop the courage to overcome those fears, we might never have the opportunity to reach our dreams and goals.

Calculating Risk and Overcoming Fear

Your ability to take risks depends on your decision-making skills and on your approach to risk. First, you have to understand what needs, desires, and values motivate your behavior. If you aren't certain of your goals and clear in your vision for your life, then you are ill-prepared to take risks that will move you toward those goals.

Before taking risks, then, check your vision and evaluate whether the risk you are considering is in line with your values. Are you considering taking the risk for good reason or for ego? Is the risk appealing to you because it will help you lead a better, more worthwhile and challenging life, or will it simply mean more money, more prestige, or more physical gratification?

Think about a risk you are considering taking, and answer these questions about it:

What lies on the other side? If you take this risk, how will it affect your goals and your vision for yourself?

———————————————————————————————

———————————————————————————————

———————————————————————————————

Will taking the risk strengthen the important areas of your life—your relationships, your educational pursuits, your personal development, and so on—or will it weaken any of these aspects?

_____

_____

_____

Why does the risk appeal to you?

_____

_____

_____

Write down what you stand to gain by taking this risk:

_____

_____

_____

Write down what you stand to lose from this risk:

_____

_____

_____

Now weigh the potential gain against the downside and ask yourself, Will this move me closer to fulfilling my vision for my life, or could it potentially set me back?

_____

_____

_____

One method for gaining the faith and confidence necessary to take on your fears is to purposely confront your fears. Here are a few questions to help you face and overcome a fear.

Identify a fear that you have—one that keeps you from taking risks that you feel you should probably take to be successful.

_____

Why is this a fear for you?

_____

_____

_____

How can you overcome this fear? Consider practical steps to take and resources and people that can offer assistance.

_____

_____

_____

Describe one action you intend to take this week to reduce the impact of this fear.

_____

_____

_____

Learning from Failure and Criticism

Identify someone you consider successful and ask that person how many failures he or she experienced before success came. I guarantee you that any successful person had to learn failure before success. That is what learning is all about: doing it wrong to get it right. We don't all succeed at everything we try. Most of us go through failure to reach success, just as we go through fear in order to build courage. As Ralph Waldo Emerson said, "Do the thing you fear, and the death of fear is certain."

Weightlifting is the simplest example I can think of to illustrate the process of going through failure to reach success. In fact, fitness instructors often talk about "going for failure." Now that sounds like fun, doesn't it? *Let's go fail!?!* What does that mean? In weightlifting, to go for failure means to push yourself to the limit, to lift as much as you can as many times as you can until you can't lift any more. Why do you do that? To build muscle, you first break it down, exhaust it, and then build new strength into it. By going for failure, you are preparing your muscles for greater success.

In life, as in weightlifting, failure is nothing more than a part of growing and building strength. Don't think of a failure as permanent. If you do that, you give failure too much power over your life. But if you put failure in its proper place, as simply a step in the Success Process, you empower yourself to take life on.

Let's say that one of your teachers names you a group leader for a class project that will span a couple of months. Halfway into the project, though, your teacher pulls you aside one Friday and says she may have to replace you as group leader because your group hasn't progressed; your project is way behind. She says you're coasting, goofing around, while the other groups are making good progress.

Ouch. That sort of criticism can make for a long weekend—or maybe not. Maybe, just maybe, it could energize you to push yourself to the outer limits of your abilities, making your teacher happy and perhaps teaching you a lesson that can expand your potential for bettering your life.

Here are three very different responses that you could have to the criticism delivered by your teacher. Which one of them is the healthiest and most beneficial?

1. **I'm worthless and I'm weak.** Your teacher's words weigh on you like a water-bed mattress dumped on your back. They get heavier and heavier as the negative thoughts flow in. *I'm in over my head. I can't lead this project. I'm a screwup.* Overwhelmed by negative thoughts, you sink into depression and spend the weekend lying on the couch and feeling sorry for yourself. When you do drag yourself back to school, your teacher sees immediately that you have not taken her words to heart and she replaces you as group leader. Your response to her criticism was self-defeating and rooted in a negative approach to life. Criticism here is viewed as the end result, the killing blow.

2. **This teacher has never liked me. I don't like how she treats me.** As soon as the teacher walks away, you throw your backpack across the room and stomp out. When you get home, you kick the cat over the neighbor's fence, hand out insults to family members like you hand out candy at Halloween, and make everyone's life miserable. Anger—seething, boiling, red-faced anger—has you in its hold. You spend the weekend building yourself into a full rage, charge into school on Monday morning like an ugly storm, and yell at the teacher for "doing you wrong." She responds by pointing the way to the principal's office. You have taken her criticism as a personal affront, and it has poisoned your judgment.

3. **What can I do to get back on track?** Instead of taking the criticism as a knife to the heart or as a personal insult, you take it as an opportunity to review and improve your performance as a group leader. *Is there truth in what my teacher said? How have I done compared to the other group leaders? What are they doing that I am not doing? What can I do to show my teacher that I am committed to improving?* You go home in a contemplative mood, sobered by the criticism, but not defeated by it. You spend the weekend doing constructive things while also weighing the best approach to the week ahead. You go back to school on Monday, tell your teacher that you have taken her criticism to heart and that you are going to

103

rededicate yourself to your duties as group leader. You have used criticism as a building block.

■ Handling Criticism

Identify a specific recent example of you being criticized by someone.

_____

_____

_____

Describe briefly but in detail your reaction—your feelings, your response, and so on.

_____

_____

_____

How would you respond to someone who reacted to criticism in the three ways just described?

1. "I'm worthless and I'm weak." _____

_____

2. "This teacher has never liked me. I don't like how she treats me." _____

_____

3. "What can I do to get back on track?" _____

_____

What happened as a result of your response?

_____

_____

_____

In hindsight, what should your response have been?

_____

_____

This journaling assignment will help you see how to effectively handle criticism, to use it for your own good.

Turning Negatives into Positives

Think back to when you learned how to ride a bike. How many times did you go out and try to ride that bike, only to fail? How many times did you skin your knees or bite the dirt? But each of those failures contributed to your eventual success, didn't they? (Don't tell me you're still riding around with the training wheels on!)

Write down a recent success that came out of failure:

_____

_____

Now, write down the failure(s) that preceded that success.

_____

_____

_____

Taking Control of Your Life

Don't allow your peers to dictate how you live your life, particularly if they have not established that they have your best interests at heart. Believe me, it is worth the risk of facing criticism and rejection if it means keeping your self-respect. Are you giving up too much to please others and to avoid criticism? I'd say you are if:

- You are trying to get people to like you rather than to respect you
- You do things you know are wrong simply to gain approval
- You do something you really don't want to do for someone who doesn't really have your best interests at heart
- It seems like you can't do enough to please someone
- A friendship or relationship seems like more work than fun

Here are five things to strive for in handling criticism, risking disapproval, and taking control of your life:

1. **Take pleasure in being in control of your own life.** Don't cater to the whims of others. Be thoughtful of other people and their needs, but only because you want to, not because they demand it. You give up too much of yourself when you forfeit control of your life to others by catering to their demands or trying to live up to their expectations rather than your own.

2. **Feel free to express your uniqueness and your own needs.** Everyone, and especially young people, face great pressure to fit in with the crowd. I encourage you to express your own talents and gifts and to celebrate them without feeling pressure to wear the same clothes, do the same things, and to follow the crowd if you don't care to. If blending in makes you feel more comfortable, fine, but don't submerge your own personality to win approval.

3. **Don't feel guilty about saying no.** You have the right to say no and the *responsibility* to say no if that is what you judge to be the proper response. You may not be correct. You may be the only one. It may make you unpopular. Nevertheless, it is your right. Have no fear, have no guilt—say no whenever and wherever you judge it to be in your best interest. They can argue with your judgment, but not with your right to make that judgment.

4. **Let them know where you stand, loudly and proudly.** Don't be afraid to take a stand or to let people know that you have taken a stand. No one respects a wishy-washy person. Don't force your opinions on other people; don't expect others to applaud every time you offer an opinion. But feel free to exercise your free will and to let others know that you are willing to take a stand even when it might not be popular.

5. **Be curious about life and all that it has to offer you.** Too often, we pull back from things that interest us for fear that we will be criticized by other people. *Classical music? That's for nerds. You're working with the handicapped? What are you, a do-gooder?* Feel free to check out the things that interest *you*. If someone else doesn't like it, that's too bad.

▓ Standing Up for Who You Are

The ability to take control of your life can help you explore and push your own outer limits. How good are you at taking control? Circle "True" or "False" for each of the following statements.

I rarely cater to the whims of others. If someone asks me to do something, I usually base my decision on whether it's right for me.

True   False

I am much more concerned about living up to my own expectations than the expectations of others.

True   False

I'm not concerned with fitting in with the "in" crowd.

True   False

I feel proud of my uniqueness and who I am as a person.

True   False

I don't give in to peer pressure. I can say no when I need to.

True   False

When I say no to something my friends want me to do and I know it was the right decision, I don't feel guilty about it.

True   False

I can take a stand on something that I feel strongly about.

True   False

I'd rather be ridiculed or rejected than do something stupid, illegal, or immoral.

True   False

I pursue my interests even if they aren't judged "cool" by others.

True   False

I try new things even if I think I might be inept at first.

True   False

Now rate yourself:

1–3 "true" answers—You're letting others control your life

4–6 "true" answers—You're gaining control of your life in some areas, but need to work on it in other areas

7–8 "true" answers—You're in good control of your life

9–10 "true" answers—You're in great control of your life and are wise and mature beyond your years!

Now that you've learned how to step into the outer limits, take well-calculated risks, and learn from failure and criticism, you're ready to take the next step: adapting to change. Most people dislike change, but you can make it work *for* you, rather than *against* you, in the Success Process. Read on.

Step 6: Pilot the Seasons of Change

If we don't change, we don't grow. If we don't grow, we are not really living. Growth demands a temporary surrender of security.

—Gail Sheehy

The Midwest, and Chicago in particular, is known to experience frequent and abrupt weather changes. "Don't like the weather? Just hang on for five minutes. It'll change." Or so the saying goes.

Change happens. It happens to everyone throughout his or her life. It happens whether you seek it or not; it happens whether you are following your vision or not; it happens whether you are stepping into your outer limits or not. What's important is how you respond to change. Don't fool yourself into thinking you can avoid it, because you can't.

You may want to feel in control of your life, but the reality is that you can't control everything. Some people have a great fear of change. Many times this is due to a fear of the unknown, of stepping outside a comfort zone, of being forced to try new things that you'd really rather not try.

So far, you have learned how to:

- Increase your self-awareness so that you are in control of your emotions and feelings and understand what your strengths are

- Create a vision of a fulfilling life
- Devise a plan to pursue that vision through goals you set
- Develop your own rules of the road to help you stay focused and to keep you from losing sight of the people and principles that are important to you
- Open up new opportunities for yourself by taking calculated risks.

Now, in this step, you'll learn how to:

- Understand the natural process of change
- Pilot the seasons, or stages, of change
- Seek change, rather than just letting it happen
- Manage change, including controlling your anger, developing patience, and handling stress

The message here is simple: to be successful, you have to learn how to adapt to change, how to not be defeated by it or fear it, how to make it work for you. To make it work for you, you first have to understand the process.

Understanding the Process of Change

Change is a part of life. Seasons change, people grow, fads come and go, dynasties crumble, beauty withers, caterpillars become butterflies, landscapes change, and on and on. You are not the same person you were a year ago; you have experienced more and, we hope, learned and grown wiser. You are honing your talents as a pianist or a point guard or a poet. You have most likely made changes, subtly or not so subtly, in your physical appearance, your emotional makeup, your spiritual grounding, your intellectual base. Change is all around you, and you are part of that change.

Not all change is unwelcome or hard to handle. For instance, maybe your past year's hard work to improve your skills as a point guard has been rewarded with a starting position. That's a change that you most likely will gladly accept—even if you have some concern about starting.

Other change, however, is harder: the loss of a loved one, the breakup of a relationship, the loss of your ability to do something you love. For instance, let's say you're that point guard who has finally earned the right to start. On the eve of the first game, you severely sprain your ankle and will be out for several games. *That* change is much harder to deal with—but no less a part of life than the more desired changes.

Sometimes, people react to changes in their life as though change is a rare and shocking experience. But our entire lives are a cycle of constant change, seasons of change, as reflected in this beautiful and familiar passage from the biblical Book of Ecclesiastes:

To every thing there is a season, and a time to every purpose under heaven:
A time to be born, and a time to die; a time to plant, and a time to pluck up
*   that which is planted;*
A time to kill, and a time to heal; a time to break down, and a time to build up;
A time to weep, and a time to laugh; a time to mourn, and a time to dance;
A time to cast away stones, and a time to gather stones together; a time to
*   embrace, and a time to refrain from embracing;*
A time to get, and a time to lose; a time to keep, and a time to cast away;
A time to rend, and a time to sew; a time to keep silence, and a time to speak;
A time to love, and a time to hate; a time of war, and a time of peace.

Navigating the Seasons of Change

Change, then, is not an event—it is a natural process, like the change of seasons in nature. The four seasons can be likened to four stages of change, during which your emotional responses may range from a sense of loss and sadness to a feeling of disorientation and lethargy to gradual rejuvenation and exhilaration. These emotions mirror, in many ways, the moods and emotions that accompany the changing seasons in nature. The four stages of change are the following:

1. Letting go of old things to welcome in new things
2. Sticking to plans to change even when you feel anxious
3. Holding tight during the ups-and-downs of change
4. Blossoming and growing through change

No doubt you've struggled through—and grown through—many changes in your life. Let's take a look at each stage of change to see how you can better adapt and use the change for your own good.

Stage One: Letting Go

Have you ever been excited about a certain change coming, yet felt sad over what was ending? That's how many people describe their high school graduation (though it's also true there are those who are not sad at all to leave high school!). These mixed emotions you may have experienced in letting go are quite common. The end of summer and the beginning of another school year often bring these mixed emotions, as does the end of a difficult class in which you made some unexpected gains. On the one hand, you breathe a sigh of relief that the class is over; but on the other hand, with your next breath you feel a strange sadness that you will be leaving the class that brought so much challenge—and growth.

How many times have you held on to habit or way of life that you knew wasn't that good for you, even when a better way was awaiting you? You want to change, yet you don't want to let go. Just as trees cut off nourishment to their leaves in the fall, the process of change begins with the act of letting go of that part of life we want to change. If the trees didn't release their old leaves, their branches would not be able to sprout buds for new growth.

It's weird, but I was afraid to change my attitude for the better. I'd sort of had this reputation as having this bad attitude, and I finally realized I was getting nowhere with it—the person I was really hurting with it was myself. So I really wanted to change, but it was like, if I change my attitude, I've lost this part of me, this part that sort of defined who I was. And that was scary. Even though I knew the change would be for the better, I felt like I was losing something that, in a way, was really valuable.

—Anita, age fifteen

Here are a few suggestions on what you can do to help yourself let go of the past in order to make positive changes in your life.

- **Tune in to your emotions.** Monitor your feelings and your attitudes toward those around you. Don't allow your emotions to cloud your judgment or to spark negative behavior.
- **Recognize that sadness and anger are common reactions to change.** There is no need to fight these feelings. That only brings more turmoil. Take the sadness or anger and channel it into positive energy by accepting it and understanding why you feel the way you do. If you are sad, do something that makes you laugh or elevates your mood. If you are angry, use that energy to do something constructive that you've been putting off, such as exercising or working on a class project.
- **Acknowledge your feelings and any sense of loss.** Put your moods into perspective and grant yourself permission to feel sad or angry or whatever you feel. There is no reason to feel guilty or angry at yourself for having perfectly valid emotions.
- **Say goodbye.** Bid farewell in your own way to the people, places, and things that will be left behind when things change. Accept what has happened, acknowledge how you feel about it, and embrace the change that has resulted.

Stage Two: Sticking to Your Plans

Oftentimes, you feel sad, stagnant, or lost shortly after you let go of something during a change. You may feel as though you have made a mistake in giving up the old and chancing something new. This is a natural reaction at this stage of the change process. Rosabeth Moss Kanter, a Harvard Business School professor and the author of *The Change Masters,* was referring to this when she wrote that "every change looks like failure in the middle."

It is natural to feel anxious when making a change. When you find yourself anxious, understand and acknowledge your anxiety, but don't despair. Stick with your plans to pursue a better life. Although you may want to give up or go back to the old way, you have to be courageous when you are chasing a dream.

Give yourself credit for having put enough thought into your decision to change *before* you took the action. This is no time for second thoughts or looking over your shoulder—this is the period for moving resolutely ahead, for keeping faith in yourself and your decision to change. Not to frighten you, but it could be disastrous to turn back on your decision at this point because you have already altered your old situation by leaving it. The way things were no longer exists. It is better to follow through and look ahead.

Stage Three: Holding on Tight

This is when your vision is put to the test. This is when you find out whether you are really on track to your dream. Everything seems accelerated, every emotion accentuated. You feel more alive than ever before. It is a time that requires thoughtful handling. Otherwise, you can get swept away by all of the rapid developments and lose focus or feel overwhelmed.

Here are some things you can do to help manage this phase of change:

- **Stop planning and get into action.** Things begin to happen now because you have laid the groundwork and made your decision. Now is the time to take advantage of the opportunities that open up. It can be daunting when change is unfolding all around you, but this is when you want to act upon your dreams.
- **Be prepared to expand your vision.** Keep in mind that you may need to adjust your vision for a better life to accommodate the growth you are undergoing. You may need to set your sights even higher than before to allow for that growth—you certainly don't want to stop one day and look back and say, "I missed that opportunity to move to an even higher level." At the very least, you want to be alert to the fact that as your opportunities grow, you need to grow too.

- **Take it step by step.** In this period of rapid change, you may be stepping along at a brisk pace, if not sprinting! Even so, keep in mind earlier lessons on setting direction for your vision so that you always stay on course.
- **Stay focused on your primary goals.** There will be many temptations and distractions at this point of the change process, so you need to remind yourself of your ultimate goal. This doesn't mean that you can't explore other opportunities, but always ask yourself whether they're taking you where you want to go with your life.
- **Take care of your life.** In such an exhilarating time, it is easy to focus on the change process and neglect other aspects of your life. Remember, however, that a balanced life includes maintaining healthy situations in your relationships, your personal development, and your school life.

Stage Four: Blossoming and Growing

During this stage of change, the focus is on continued growth. Here are some ideas to guide you:

- **Check your bearings.** Are you proceeding in line with your needs, desires, and values? Or have you become distracted and lured off the path? What do you need to do to get on track and stay there? Consider where you need to head on the next leg of your journey to a better life. Let the seeds of your plan emerge now so that over the next few seasons they can take root.
- **Write out your current options.** Note which ones provide the greatest opportunity for growth in the areas that are important to you. Cross off those that take you in tempting directions that are not in line with your principles, values, and general guidelines for living.
- **Confide in your closest friends.** How do they see your decisions and actions for change? Are they with you, or do they think you have strayed off the path that is best for you?

■ Stages of Change

One of the risks you need to take to be successful is to embrace change. We all face some changes that we can't control; many of us, for instance, resist the idea of having to move to a different neighborhood, city, or school. But we can't let the fear of change—any change—prevent us from being successful. We have to learn how to manage the changes in our lives—to take advantage of the opportunities we have to make changes for the better or to make changes work for us.

We broke down the process of change into four stages: letting go, sticking to your plans, holding on tight, and blossoming and growing. Answer the following questions about each stage. But before you do, think a moment about a change that you feel would be good for you to make in your life, but one that would be difficult for you to make. It could be a behavior, a thought pattern, an attitude, a way of life. Keep in mind a change that will help you toward your vision.

Got it? OK. Look into the future, visualize, and answer these questions about the change that you have in mind.

▦ Stage One: Letting Go

What are the things you will have to give up in order to make the change you want?

_____

_____

_____

Will these things be hard to give up? If so, why?

_____

_____

_____

How would you feel if you let go of them?

_____

_____

_____

What would help you let go of them?

_____

_____

_____

What would happen if you let go of them?

_____

_____

_____

What would happen if you *don't* let go of them?

_____

_____

_____

■ Stage Two: Sticking to Your Plans

Now imagine that you have let go of the things you needed to in order to make the change. You are now in the midst of making the change. How do you feel? Why?

_____

_____

_____

If you're feeling anxious or are worried about the change and whether you can do it, what will help you focus on the positive and keep going?

_____

_____

_____

What tends to pull you down or makes you feel uncertain about your decisions to change?

_____

_____

_____

When are you most tempted to give up on a change, even if you think it's for the better?

_____

_____

_____

What motivates you to continue on with a change, even if you're feeling a bit shaky or uncertain?

_____

_____

_____

▨ **Stage Three: Holding on Tight**

You've stuck to your plans so far. Good job! You're beginning to adapt to your change. But you're still experiencing ups and downs in this stage. How good are you at managing the ups and downs of change? Are you adaptable and flexible?

_____

_____

_____

During this stage you often are moved from a passive to an active role in change or from thinking about change to actually making change happen in your life. Do you have trouble going from thinking about doing something to actually doing it? If so, why?

_____

_____

_____

You often make rapid, but at times erratic, progress in this stage. If you stumble or make a bad decision in your change, what do you do?

_____

_____

_____

Why is it important to stay focused on your primary goals during this stage?

_____

_____

_____

■ Stage Four: Blossoming and Growing

Congratulations! You've successfully made a change in your life. How does it feel having made that change?

_____

_____

_____

How is your life better?

_____

_____

_____

What other areas of growth or opportunities might open up as a result of this change you made?

_____

_____

_____

Seeking Change

Some change is forced upon you by external circumstances. Other change you bring about yourself to create opportunities. Quite often these types of change blend good with bad.

How you approach change is crucial to your ability to adapt to and use change as a learning experience and means to improve your life. If you are to seek a better life than the one you have now, you have to _make your own changes_ and not just wait for good things to happen to you. You have to stop just going along and getting along and start chasing your dreams and challenging life. That takes courage. Seeking and dealing with change, even positive change, requires self-control, patience, and perseverance. Change can emotionally overwhelm you to the point that your power to reason is diminished and your vision of a better life is clouded.

Remember the stage of change I described as "letting go"? If you can't let go of something, it's hard to seek change—even if you want it badly. It's like trying to drive with the parking brake on: you want to go, but you're being held back.

Albert Einstein once said, "The significant problems we face cannot be solved at the same level of thinking we were at when we created them." You can't always find the answers within your existing environment; sometimes you have to seek change, or at least change your perspective, in order to find answers.

Managing Change

Sometimes even minor changes in your life can trigger strong feelings. Say your car breaks down on the way to school one day. It puts you in a foul mood for that day and for the rest of the week while you have to take a bus to school—you detest getting on the bus after experiencing the freedom of driving by yourself. Or, during summer, your best friend goes off to camp or on vacation. Suddenly your daily routine is altered, and you sulk around the house and scowl—you don't know what to do with yourself.

Bigger changes evoke even stronger emotions and feelings. Your parents get divorced. Your older sister has a baby. Your father loses his job. Your young nephew dies. Your older brother wins the lottery (that's the good news) and suddenly seems not to recognize you (that's the bad news). Such unexpected events carry with them intense feelings that may interfere with your ability to function.

> If you are to seek a better life than the one you have now, you have to *make your own changes* and not just wait for good things to happen to you.

I thought the guy was a creep, if you want to know the truth. I didn't want a stepdad. I had a real dad. Even if he wasn't living in our house anymore, I had a father. The thought of my stepfather moving into our house made me physically sick. I was really mad at my mom.

—Jessica, age fourteen

A key point here is that just as change is natural, so are those feelings that accompany it. Jessica is expressing her anger at her parents getting divorced and the resulting changes. There's nothing wrong with her feelings. But along with those feelings, she needs to learn how to manage that change to make it work for her.

We all need to learn how to manage change. In the next few pages we'll focus on three ways to do so: by controlling anger, developing patience, and handling stress. If you can do these three things, you're well on your way to managing change.

Controlling Your Anger

Here are five tips for controlling anger in times of change:

1. **Step back and look at the big picture.** Anger is a natural response. In times of danger or stress, anger triggers increased blood flow and adrenaline prepares people for flight or fight. This response serves a purpose, but you want to make sure it serves *your* purpose. Are you directing your anger at the real source of your resentment? And even if you have the right target, are you hurting yourself? Don't sabotage yourself because of fleeting anger. Put the anger aside and assess the situation. If your anger is being vented in a self-destructive manner, find another way to let it out.

2. **Remove yourself from the scene of the crime.** If a change has triggered powerful feelings of anger and resentment, make a strategic retreat. Take that anger somewhere and let it out through a run or put it into a punching bag (just make sure it's a real bag and not a person!). Use that energy; don't suppress it. But use it wisely, away from the situation that made you angry in the first place.

3. **Transform negative emotions to positive action.** If you are angry with a teacher because that teacher doesn't see your potential, use that energy to excel in class and prove the teacher wrong. If you are angry at a friend who has betrayed a secret of yours, use the energy to become more trustworthy yourself. Don't be hurtful or vengeful; do something positive to ease your anger and to gain perspective.

4. **Talk it out.** Talk with friends or family members who are not immediately involved in whatever is triggering your anger. Go somewhere away from the scene of the crime and talk through your anger to avoid saying things or doing things that will only hurt you or your cause.

5. **Take stock of your options.** Many times, anger results from feeling trapped and robbed of opportunities, but in truth, your anger may be blinding you to the opportunities that await. It has been said that in times of change, people concentrate far too much on the door that has been closed instead of looking for doors that have been opened. Rather than being swept up emotionally, charge up mentally and consider what opportunities might have opened up by the change that has triggered your anger. Now is the time to act, not react.

Developing Patience

You cannot shortcut your way through the change process. You must expect change to throw you off somewhat, that it will take adapting to. People who aren't very patient can give up on change before they can experience the benefits from it. If you're like this, you're going through a lot of pain for nothing, because you're turning back before you get to the promised land. Expect bumps and jolts along the way, but ride them through. The way you do that is with patience.

Let's say you're really interested in music and you decide that you want to play in a band with some friends or in the school band. However, you've never played an instrument before. Needless to say, you have your work cut out for you. You will have to change your daily routine, because you'll need to practice daily. And once the thrill of getting your own instrument wears off, and the reality of the work sets in, it won't be easy. For those of you who have played guitar, do you remember what it was like those first few weeks and months? Your fingertips can get so sore and callused that they can crack and bleed. You probably never realized there were so many nerve endings in one tiny place! It takes patience to stick with learning something new, to change behavior, or to adapt to new circumstances. And if you are learning guitar and you give it up after three months, you have only some sore fingers and a lot of wasted practice time to show for it.

It's no wonder many people struggle with being patient. In our world, we want immediate solutions to problems, we want immediate results, and we often get them, so we aren't always willing to put in the time or energy to get solutions and results when they don't come instantly. If you want to get a step ahead of most people in taking on change and making it work for you, then develop patience. Don't be so quick to judge a change or give up on it (or on yourself). Good things don't always come quickly. Some change takes time. Give it the time it needs and you may be quite surprised—and pleased—with the results.

Handling Stress

The process of change can be stressful, even when changes are for the better. You need a game plan for handling that stress. Here are five tips for dealing with the stress of change:

1. **Stay focused on your dream for a better life.** Sure, you may hit hard times when you make a change. Your friends may criticize you; you may doubt yourself. It may be exhausting to do all that is required to get to the next level of achievement or preparation. I never said it would be easy. But you can ease some of the stress by not focusing on how hard it is. Instead, keep in mind how much better it will be when you have completed this change.

2. **Stay true to your principles and beliefs.** Doing things that go against your beliefs and values can trigger stress. The process of change can test those basic beliefs, and, occasionally, you may find that you have compromised your beliefs. You may find yourself being untruthful or in other situations that you would not normally have to contend with. This is stressful because you are violating your own rules. To avoid this stress, do your best to stay within your normal guidelines for behavior. Be aware that even temporarily abandoning those guidelines will have serious and stressful consequences.

3. **Give yourself a break.** Understand that stress comes with change and compensate for that by giving yourself a break. Take time out from the usual routine to reduce stress and mental fatigue. Do things that recharge you emotionally, physically, intellectually, and spiritually. Stress saps energy; you need to renew that energy.

4. **Unload your calendar.** Times of change are not times to take on more projects or challenges that will add to your stress load. Don't burn the candle at both ends; take time to relax. When you are undergoing change in one part of your life, try to keep the other areas of your life under control. Take on no more than one major stressor at a time, if possible. Put off nonessential changes for later.

5. **Put out your dis-stress signals.** Far too many people are unwilling to ask for help when they're stressed. Why have friends and family if you can't lean on them in hard times? I take it as a compliment when friends need support and come to me. It makes me feel needed and valuable in their lives. You don't want to overdo it, but in critical times, put out the signal that you need some support.

▪ Changing Your Way of Thinking

Three keys to adapting to change are controlling your anger, developing patience, and handling stress. Change brings with it a wealth of emotions; it can at times be like a roller-coaster ride. Answer the following questions to examine how well you adapt to change and how anger, patience, and stress affect your ability to change.

Think about a recent change in your life—a move to a new home, for instance, or a change in your classes or extracurricular activities, or a change in a personal relationship.

Write down the change that occurred.

_____

_____

_____

How did you feel about this change?

_____

_____

_____

The things I liked about the change were . . .

_____

_____

_____

The things I didn't like about the change were . . .

_____

_____

_____

Were you surprised by your reactions?

_____

_____

_____

Overall, do you now regard the change as a positive or negative experience?

_____

_____

_____

Based on how things turned out, do any of the fears, concerns, or negative emotions that you experienced now seem justified?

_____

_____

_____

Do you think you could have managed your response to the change better?

_____

_____

_____

■ Anger, Patience, and Stress

What types of change might make you angry?

_____

_____

_____

Why?

_____

_____

_____

Has anger ever negatively affected how you adapted to what turned out to be a positive change in your life?

_____

_____

_____

What can you do to turn any anger you might feel when you face your next big change into something positive?

_____

_____

_____

Are you normally a patient person when it comes to important things or do you tend to give up on things quickly?

_____

_____

_____

What types of things are you willing to be patient about?

_____

_____

_____

How can patience help you achieve your goals?

_____

_____

_____

Think of a time when you were stressed by a big change going on in your life. What was your response to that change?

_____

_____

_____

If you could go back and do things differently, would you respond differently to that change? If so, how?

_____

_____

_____

What are ways that you can unload stress and relax?

_____

_____

_____

There's no doubt about it—change is a constant in our lives. By learning to let go of things and sticking to your plan, you can begin to make change work for you. Learning how to control your anger, develop patience, and handle stress are three keys that will help you adapt to change and use it for your own good.

One important way to handle stress is to ask for help from others, rather than carrying the burden alone. Support from others is a key to your success—no one truly makes it on his or her own. What you need to do is build your own "dream team." We'll explore how to do that in the next step.

Step 7: Build Your Dream Team

Self-realization would not be achieved one by one, but all together or not at all.

—W. E. B. DuBois

Turning your dream into reality doesn't happen easily. Many people think they can, or even *should*, try to go it alone as they pursue their dreams and goals. The truth is, however, if you want meaningful, long-term success, you need others to help you achieve it. Success comes not only through your own efforts, but also through assistance, guidance, and encouragement from many others—it doesn't matter if you're talking about small, personal success or victories where the whole world takes notice.

It may sound romantic to go it alone, but flying solo is not an effective way to approach the Success Process. In fact, *no one* makes it alone; building and maintaining mutually supportive relationships is *essential* if you are to successfully pursue a better life.

In this step, then, we'll explore four areas essential to building the types of relationships that can help you realize your dreams. We'll look at how you can:

- Use teamwork to reach goals
- Forge positive partnerships
- Build trust
- Grow your support team

Using Teamwork to Reach Goals

A key element of the Success Process is building relationships with people who care about you and believe in your goals. As you grow and expand the possibilities for your life, having relationships that strengthen you is vital. How many people do you know who have been urged on by those people around them to develop their talents and to succeed? I know many, many people like that. I also know people who have had difficulty building better lives for themselves because they didn't have anyone in their corner cheering them on, advising them, and helping them to get through the hard times.

Think in terms of your own experience. Have you accomplished your proudest achievements entirely on your own or with the support, help, and encouragement of others? Team sports are an obvious example of the teamwork it takes to reach goals, but for *every* achievement, there is some type of support system behind it. And this support system works both ways—that is, while at times you will need that support and help for yourself, at other times you will be supporting and helping others. That's what teamwork is about: banding together to help one another reach goals. Whether you realize it or not, you are part of a team—or, more likely, several loose-knit teams.

Forging Positive Partnerships

So, how do you choose your dream team wisely? Successful teams—be they formal or informal, a group of twenty or of two—have these five characteristics in common:

1. They are committed to a common goal
2. They share common values and expectations
3. Their members play roles that complement one another
4. They have a plan for confronting and solving problems
5. They have a plan for evaluating progress

Let's take a closer look at each characteristic.

Teams Have Common Goals

The first key is for everyone on the "team" to agree on goals. If you don't share the same goals, it's impossible to decide how to work together to achieve them. Listen to this testimony:

> My brother and I argued for about an hour, back and forth, back and forth, until suddenly I just sort of sat back and smiled. This just made him all the madder. "What's so funny?" he asked. I said, "We're arguing for the same thing. We want the same thing. We just want Mom to be happy, that's all." Mom had just got remarried and we didn't agree on whether she should have or not. But we both wanted the same thing: we wanted her to be happy. After that we calmed down a little.
>
> —Steve, age sixteen

Sharing common goals is at the center of positive relationships. Rather than wasting energy trying to explain your goals or win people over, you can gain energy from like-minded people who not only understand your goals, but also feel the same way about them that you do. Sharing common goals can act as glue when trouble arises, because you all know that you are after the same thing. Common goals can hold teams together when they encounter problems.

Teams Share Common Values and Expectations

People on winning teams share common expectations about how all team members should behave, including agreement on what role each member is expected to play. This goes for any team you put together, too. Your family and friends might help you reach personal goals. Teachers and counselors can help you reach education goals. In both cases, each person contributes something of value to the effort; each one shares the core values that are behind the effort, and each one knows the role he or she can play to help you achieve your goal.

In musical groups, direction for the team is provided by the musical score. On your team, you and the team members set the direction. You agree upon expected behavior based upon the group's values. People who hold greatly differing values are likely to have very different ideas about appropriate behavior in the relationship, and thus they won't provide much lasting support.

Team Members Play Complementary Roles

Musicians must decide which instrument each member of the band will play and which part the vocalists will sing. So too people involved in successful partnerships know what part each will play in achieving their mutually agreed-upon goals.

Clarity about roles is essential. It gives your team the information it needs about how each member fits into the game plan, what they can expect from one another, and how their roles interact. If each person's role is not clearly defined, conflict is likely.

For instance, let's say that no one in your family has graduated from college before, but you have plans to not only graduate from college but to perhaps attain an advanced degree. Members of your support team can and should play distinct roles. For example:

- Your family offers encouragement
- Your teachers help shape your educational goals
- Your career counselor guides you in career and college choices
- A friend might tutor you (or you might be involved in a study group with friends with similar goals)
- A family acquaintance or a mentor who is in the field you are interested in offers guidance and insight
- Your parents, in addition to offering encouragement and emotional support, also provide financial support and apply for financial aid to help you reach your goal
- A few close friends offer emotional support and encouragement

Everyone plays a distinct part, and together, the support, guidance, and encouragement offered is significant.

Teams Confront and Solve Problems

Conflict is a part of life. Even on the closest of teams, disagreements will occur. You need to find ways to resolve conflicts so that the team always moves forward rather than gets hung up on internal problems. Can you imagine a musical performance in which members of the band stop playing because they can't agree on how to interpret a song? How about a basketball team so torn apart by jealousies and misunderstandings that they can't compete?

If you're part of a group or team that has a conflict it cannot solve, one of two things happens: either you hobble along in a crippled state, achieving far less than you reasonably should, or you disband altogether. In fact, part of the strength of a healthy team is that it can solve problems and achieve more together when it works through the hard times.

For instance, in keeping with the last example, let's say your desire to graduate from college is meeting with opposition from your mother. She is not against higher education, but she is concerned about the family's financial situation and can't see how this new financial burden can be added. She is already working two part-time jobs as it is, and your father is working a full-time job—and they are barely making ends meet. In a healthy situation, you can confront and solve the problem by following these six steps:

1. **Define the problem.** The first step in resolving conflict is to decide together what the problem is. That means identifying areas of disagreement and agreement. In this case, the problem is that you want to go to college, and while your mother agrees that this is a worthy goal, she feels that the family cannot afford the financial burden.

2. **Diagnose the causes of the problem.** Next, it is important to understand what led to the conflict. Conflict can be caused by many things, including actions or events, comments (or rumors of comments made), or conflicting goals. Sometimes it helps to bring in a neutral third party to help sort through conflicting information. The cause of the conflict here is worry about family finances.

3. **Generate possible solutions.** Identify possible resolutions of the conflict and actions each person can take to achieve the resolution. For instance, you and your mother can look into various grants and forms of financial aid available, and your parents can assess the family budget to see if money could be set apart to either begin or increase an already-existing budget for education. Other possible solutions would be to go to a junior college for two years before transferring to a more expensive four-year college or university, or to go to school part-time and work part-time.

4. **Decide on a mutually acceptable solution.** Consider the effects of various solutions and select the option most acceptable to the parties involved. In this case, perhaps you decide to attend a reputable junior college while working part-time and applying for scholarships and grants to be used when you transfer to a four-year college.

5. **Implement the solution.** Once the parties involved have agreed on a solution, they should all be involved in implementing it. Continuing with our example, you would attend junior college, work part-time, and apply for scholarships and grants at the appropriate time.

6. **Evaluate the results.** All parties involved should evaluate how well the solution solved the problem. If it didn't solve the problem, seek another solution. In this case, you would evaluate both the usefulness of the junior college in terms of it helping you meet your educational goals, and your success in raising enough money and financial aid to later transfer to a four-year college.

Teams Evaluate Progress

Successful teams have ways to evaluate how much progress they are making. Teammates agree on the goal itself as well as on ways to measure progress.

Some goals are simple and clear-cut. For most teams in sports, for example, the goal is to win games. Evaluation of progress is simple: if the team wins, it has reached its immediate goal and is advancing toward a long-term goal; if it loses, it is not making progress.

Other goals are not so simple or clear-cut and therefore can be more difficult to evaluate. That's all the more reason to agree upon measurable checkpoints along the way.

When you undertake this five-step process to forge positive relationships—committing to a common goal, sharing common values and expectations, playing complementary roles, confronting and solving problems, and evaluating progress—you also are taking a step toward another important aspect of building your dream team: building trust. After you complete the following worksheet, we'll look at ways to build trust.

■ Teaming Up to Win

Relationships that are positive and make you stronger are critical to your ability to achieve your goals. Some partnerships are more successful than others. Identify a person who has had a positive influence on you in your pursuit of a goal.

Your positive teammate:

_____

_____

Identify one thing that worked well in this relationship.

Possible responses might include:

- *We got along well*
- *My teammate was very supportive*
- *We communicated well*
- *We were always able to solve problems*
- *We agreed on what we should do and how we were going to do it*
- *We trusted each other completely*
- *We agreed on what was most important*

_____

_____

_____

Identify one thing that did not work well in a different relationship.

Possible responses might be:

- *We couldn't agree on what to do*
- *We had very different methods*
- *I didn't trust this teammate*
- *I had to do all the work*
- *We didn't communicate very well*

_____

_____

_____

Think of a time when you pursued a goal. It could be the goal you have focused on for the preceding few questions, or it could be a different goal. Consider the teammate or teammates who were on your team for this goal. Assess how successful you were in the five key characteristics of forging positive partnerships by answering the following questions.

Was everyone on the team committed to the same goal? If not, why not?

_____

_____

If some people were not committed to the same goal, what was the result?

_____

_____

Did everyone on the team share common values and expectations?

_____

_____

If not, what was the result of that conflict?

_____

_____

Did each person know his or her role on the team?

_____

_____

133

If not, did conflict result from this confusion?

_____

_____

Was the team good at problem-solving?

_____

_____

Did your team have a way to evaluate your progress toward the goal?

_____

_____

If not, how would a means of evaluation have helped you?

_____

_____

In the next activity, you'll be placed in a "desperate situation" and will be forced to choose the two people who will be most valuable in helping you succeed in that situation. This will get you in a frame of mind to think about building your dream team.

■ Stranded on a Desert Island

You are lost on a deserted island in the middle of the Pacific Ocean. You have no idea how long you will be on the island. There are resources—food, water, and trees—but you have no information as to where the nearest island is or in what direction there is civilization. From the following list of people, circle the two that you would like to be stranded with on the island. Any one person may serve only one role—for example, a relative can only serve as a relative, not as a doctor as well.

- Your best friend
- A clergyman
- Any one relative of your choice
- A doctor
- A tailor
- A carpenter
- A wilderness-survival expert
- A famous actor or actress

- A sports star
- A chef
- Other _____

Explain why you chose the two people that you did.

_____

_____

_____

_____

Why should these two people want to be stranded on the island with you? What unique talents do you bring to the team?

_____

_____

_____

_____

Describe life on the island after six months.

_____

_____

_____

_____

_____

_____

Building Trust

So you want the support and encouragement of others around you, but no one is there for you? That could be the case for a lot of reasons: Perhaps you're not very open with other people so they don't know you well enough to know where you need help. Maybe you are good at asking for help but never bother to return the favor when asked. Or maybe others see in you an attitude that says "I don't care" or "I don't need anybody's help,"

TIPS FOR INSPIRING
TRUST

☑ DO WHAT YOU SAY YOU WILL DO

☑ LISTEN WITHOUT JUDGMENT

☑ BE THERE

☑ PAY WHAT YOU OWE WHEN IT IS DUE

☑ ACT HONORABLY EVEN WHEN TEMPTED OR CRITICIZED

and if *you* don't care, they surely won't. Or perhaps it's because you haven't proven yourself trustworthy. You won't be able to build much of a support team if you gossip behind your friends' backs or take things from them or don't keep your word.

Trust is not easily earned. Just look around you. How many people do you truly trust with your possessions, to protect your privacy, to keep a secret, or to tell you the truth no matter what? The list probably isn't too long.

Real trust is established over time, through shared experiences and a pattern of reliability. The process begins in childhood. Although a child may be blindly dependent early on, even toddlers become wary of family members who prove to be unreliable or hurtful. If a child learns early on that his or her own parents and siblings cannot be trusted, odds are he or she will have difficulty establishing trusting relationships or being trustworthy for the rest of his or her life.

There are all sorts of books that tell you how to appear trustworthy and sympathetic and honest, but in reality, having good character is the only way to earn the lasting trust and support of others. You don't just go out and buy good character. Nor do you develop it overnight. Again, it comes with a pattern of behavior, a way of living your life by certain rules based on age-old principles as basic and as enduring as the Golden Rule.

There is risk involved in trusting others. Not all relationships involve the same degree of trust, but trust is the key to building relationships and support teams. Trusting others can have both positive and negative consequences, and those consequences depend on how your team members respond to situations as you progress in the Success Process. You have to be able to read others' motives. Everyone has an agenda, a personal goal that may or may not be compatible with yours. You can't expect others to give your concerns and goals priority over theirs. The key is to find people whose goals are *compatible* with yours.

Behaving in a trustworthy manner—as opposed to just talking a good game—is important in building trust. There are other ways to inspire others to trust you, too. Here are eleven character traits that inspire trust.

1. **Do what you say you will do.** It's amazing how many people fail to live up to their promises yet still expect people to trust them. Again, you may fool some people for a while, but eventually the crowds will thin and you'll be left making false promises to thin air. On the other hand, if you consistently live up to the expectations that you create, you may have to build an arena to accommodate the crowds that want to line up on your side.

2. **Listen without judgment.** If a friend says she has something to tell you and she seems shameful or fearful, listen without judging her. There is no greater favor you can do for someone than to be a devoted and trusted listener. Not an advisor or counselor, but simply a listener. Give your friend your full attention and allow her to state the situation or express her emotions. Don't interrupt, don't be distracted, don't try to give her a solution while she is talking. Let her talk without her fearing what your thoughts are on the matter.

3. **Be there.** The importance of being there cannot be overstated. A friend told me that he recently filled in for a neighbor couple who had to leave town on the night of their son's school recital. He knew this boy, a second grader, fairly well, but had not spent a great deal of time alone with him. He did know, however, that it was important for the boy to have a familiar face in the crowd. The boy didn't say much on the way to the recital, and he didn't appear to care that this fellow was going to watch him perform. But when he took the stage, the first thing that boy did was scan the crowd for his neighbor's face. When he saw it, he lit up. The neighbor was where he said he would be: he knew how important it would be to the boy. That says more about the character of this man than any claims he might make.

4. **Pay what you owe when it is due.** This sounds almost revolutionary in a time of credit cards and delayed-payment plans, but in personal transactions there is

137

nothing that builds trust faster than paying debts promptly. And this goes not only for money, but for your word and for giving back what you owe in relationships too.

5. **Act honorably even when tempted or criticized.** It is easy to be an honorable person if there is no temptation or if your honor is never challenged. But how honorable are you if you have access to test answers or if you are unfairly criticized by someone who has the knack for getting your goat? Perhaps you know people in school who cheat regularly and get away with it. Likely you would never trust these people in a critical situation because their honor runs no deeper than a scratch. The most important thing is to be honest with yourself first. Are you comfortable with your own integrity? It is vital to demonstrate integrity, to stand up for your beliefs, and to resist pressure to do what you know to be wrong.

6. **Tell the truth about yourself and others.** Some people seem to be addicted to gossiping, spreading rumors, and outright lying about others. When you hear someone say something that you know isn't true, what happens? Their credibility with you is shot. You don't know if you can believe anything else they say—and you may wonder what they say about you when you're not around.

7. **Guard what is entrusted to you.** In trusting relationships, people share their greatest fears or most embarrassing moments because they trust each other. To do this with someone you do not know well is to expose yourself to criticism or rejection.

8. **Be a source of strength.** If you want to have people to lean on in your troubled times, you have to be a source of strength for them when they are in need. No one is strong all of the time, but even the weakest of us can provide support to those who trust and rely on us.

9. **Acknowledge your mistakes.** The person who is willing to admit mistakes and imperfections is more likely to inspire confidence than one who never acknowledges being wrong or having weaknesses. Why? Because we all make mistakes and we all *know* we make mistakes. But many people go to great lengths to pretend they never make mistakes. The three most difficult words for some people to say are *I was wrong*. Who do you trust more, the person who always has an answer or an excuse, or the one who acknowledges his or her limits and errors?

10. **Help others without looking for praise or payment.** Help people without seeking something in return. If you're helping a younger kid learn math theorems because you want to go out with his older sister, chances are good that the girl is going to see right through you. If, however, you take a genuine interest in the younger boy and truly offer to help him, chances are the girl is going to see something very good in you—and who knows? It may inspire her to want to go out with you. Help others without looking for rewards and the rewards will probably find you anyway.

11. **Put the welfare of others before your own.** To engender trust, show that you are as concerned about other people as you are about yourself. When other people know

you have their best interests at heart, they'll trust you in the deepest matters, because few people place the well-being of others ahead of, or even on a par with, their own well-being.

▧ In Whom Do You Trust?

Make a list of the people on your dream team, those whom you trust to guard prized possessions, to protect your privacy, to keep a secret, and to tell the truth no matter what. Next to each name, write down what makes each of them trustworthy.

_____   _____

_____   _____

_____   _____

_____   _____

_____   _____

_____   _____

Now, write down the names of people who might trust *you* in similar situations and what characteristics *you* have that make you trustworthy to each of them.

_____   _____

_____   _____

_____   _____

_____   _____

_____   _____

_____   _____

Are the same names on both lists?

_____

How difficult was it to figure out what it is about another person that inspires your trust in him or her? Why was it difficult (or easy)?

_____

_____

What about identifying your own characteristics that result in others trusting you—was that hard to do? How did it make you feel?

_____

_____

On a scale of 1 to 10 points, with 1 being very poor, 5 being average, and 10 being excellent, rate yourself on the eleven traits that inspire trust.

You do what you say you will do   _____

You listen without judgment   _____

You are there for your friends   _____

You pay what you owe, be it money, your word, whatever you owe others,
    when it is due   _____

You act honorably even when tempted or criticized   _____

You tell the truth about yourself and others   _____

You guard what is entrusted to you   _____

You are a source of strength for others when they need you   _____

You acknowledge your mistakes   _____

You help others without looking for praise or payment   _____

You put others' welfare before your own   _____

Score:

11–55	poor
56–77	average
78–88	good
89–110	excellent

Growing Your Support Team

Relationships require good communication, and they also require maintenance. If you take them for granted, they will wither and die. If you abuse them, they will fall apart. To build trusting, supportive relationships, keep these five tips in mind—a few of them reinforce what you learned earlier about teamwork.

1. **Be the host, not the guest, in the relationship.** A host is concerned about the guest's needs, interests, and point of view. If you're in a relationship where everything is "me, me, me," where the only needs you're concerned about are your own, then the relationship won't last long. Be attentive to the people who are part of your

support team. Be there for them as much as you expect them to be there for you. Build trust by showing that you want to be an active force for good in that person's life.

2. **Pay attention to the details.** A couple I know visited the home of a famous person not long ago. The host wined and dined my friends graciously, but what impressed my friends the most were the little things that this host did. "She personally put together a tray of goodies for our nightstand and saw to it that we had comfortable pillows," my friends reported. "She seemed to take a great deal of pride and interest in being a good host." It is the little things that often make the greatest impression; when you are building a trusting relationship, attention to the details can mean a lot. Remember special occasions and birthdays. Be alert to events and changes in the other person's life. Do so because you are truly involved and interested, because that is the only way to build trust.

3. **Honor all commitments, big and small, spoken and unspoken.** Few things can build or tear down trust as quickly as keeping, or failing to keep, commitments. If you intend to build a trusting relationship with someone, be there when you say you will be there. Be prepared to honor the unspoken commitments. When my father died recently, the people I trust and depend on the most stepped forward. I did not have to ask for their support, there was no spoken commitment that they would be there for me in times of sadness in my life, but I knew they would be there and they were. Those people have made a commitment to our relationship that is based on far more than their own self-interest.

4. **Live up to your own expectations.** Have you ever known someone who expected others to live by rules and principles that he or she openly ignored? That is what I am referring to when I say that you should live up to your own expectations. You cannot expect people to invest more in you than you are willing to invest in them. If you don't remember their birthdays, don't expect them to send a cake for yours. If you don't show up to celebrate their victories and successes or to console them in their setbacks, don't expect them to rush to your side on those occasions. If you expect members of your team to live with integrity, you had better be a model of it yourself. Nothing wears away trust as quickly as someone who does not practice what he preaches.

5. **Admit your mistakes.** It is going to happen: you will do something thoughtless or reckless that hurts someone who has trusted you and been there for you. The worst thing you can do is to take someone on your support team for granted and assume that they will give you the benefit of the doubt. If you screw up, if you hurt someone through thoughtless action, go to the person you have wronged and make it right. Otherwise, don't expect the relationship to continue.

▪ How Supportive Are You?

Building your dream team is a two-way street—you need to be there to support and encourage your friends if you want to expect support from them. The best team situations occur when everyone plays a role and teammates are mutually supportive of one another.

Based on the five tips for growing your support team, see how supportive you are by answering the following questions.

Think of two or three key relationships you have with people—the relationships that you feel are most supportive and helpful to you. Are these relationships mutually beneficial or are they slanted toward your needs only?

_____

_____

How do you feel when someone leans on you for support and you are able to come through and meet his or her needs?

_____

_____

Are you able to pick up on issues in your friends' lives, issues that they may need support on? Do you pay attention to the details in your friends' lives?

_____

_____

Are you able to keep your word to someone, even if it means you have to sacrifice something? Can you recall a time when you did keep your word even when it was hard for you to do so? What happened?

_____

_____

How did you feel in that situation? Were you glad you were able to keep your word or did you resent having to do it?

_____

_____

How do you think your friend felt about you keeping your word even though it meant you had to sacrifice something?

_____

_____

Do you expect more from your friends than you expect from yourself?

_____

_____

If you do expect more from your friends than from yourself, how do you think this makes your friends feel?

_____

_____

Think of a time when you made a mistake that hurt a relationship and you didn't admit your mistake. What was the result with the relationship?

_____

_____

Now think of a time when you made a hurtful mistake but were big enough to admit it. How did your admission affect the relationship?

_____

_____

The good news you learned from this step is that you don't have to go it alone in the Success Process—in fact, you really *can't* go it alone and be very successful. Instead, you need to cultivate solid, trusting relationships with a variety of people who can support you as you work toward your goals. And you have to be supportive of those who need you, too. Achievements are greater and more lasting when accomplished through a team effort, be it with a formal team, as in sports or clubs, or an informal team, such as family, friends, and mentors.

Next, we'll look at another crucial aspect of the Success Process: the ability to make good decisions. The difference between success and setback often lies in the decisions made along the way.

Step 8: Win by a Decision

Our lives are the sum total of the choices we have made.

—Wayne Dyer

The ability to make decisions to better your life is crucial to the Success Process. If you can't make decisions and take action, you won't break free and create opportunities where none appeared to exist.

You will face decisions today, tomorrow, and throughout your life. Many of these decisions can alter your life for better or worse, so your ability to make good decisions will directly affect your life. In this step you'll learn how to:

- Shape your life through your decisions
- Recognize good and bad decisions
- Realize when you are procrastinating and learn how to stop it
- Make good decisions a habit
- Use both your mind and your heart—logic and emotion—in making good decisions
- Follow a process that will help you make good decisions throughout your life

We'll begin with the big picture first: shaping your life through decisions.

Shaping Your Life Through Your Decisions

Even if you master all of the steps that we have covered so far, you will fall short in your efforts to seek a better life if you have difficulty making decisions. You might have goals and a vision for where you want to go, and you might have a plan, and you might possess the courage to take risks and make changes. But if you don't have a method for making good decisions, you'll find yourself stumbling again and again.

Some people are afraid to make decisions because they are afraid to move from what is known into the unknown. Some fear the decision-making process because it exposes them to criticism and evaluation—and they don't want to be wrong, ever. You must get past this. Yet although decision-making is such an important skill, we receive little training in how to go about it.

What you are in this world is largely the result of the decisions you make. That's right—the decisions *you* make. No one else can make the important decisions for you, and no one else *should* make them for you. You are not the victim of circumstances that happen *to* you; you are the maker of decisions that can work *for* you. You are free to make your decisions. You have that right. You have the power to choose by making decisions. If you are not happy with where you are in life, or if you think you can do better, then you can decide to do something different.

We all have the ability to change our lives at any time—whether that means going from something bad to something good, or from something good to something even better.

Recognizing Good and Bad Decisions

How do you know if you are making good decisions in your life? Here are some characteristics of good decisions. Good decisions . . .

- Open opportunities
- Make you feel good about yourself
- Allow you to express your talents, skills, and knowledge
- Silence your critics
- Move you closer to your goals
- Keep you focused on the future
- Reduce your frustrations and anger
- Increase your potential
- Attract dynamic people to your cause

How do you know if you are making bad decisions? Here are some characteristics of bad decisions. Bad decisions . . .

- Put you on a dead-end street
- Result in second thoughts
- Cause you to look over your shoulder
- Inspire feelings of regret
- Lure critics
- Bring trouble to your life
- Attract predators who hope to capitalize on more bad decisions

Obviously, if you want to pursue a better life, you need a process for making good decisions. Big decisions require big thinking. Often, the only difference between you and someone you admire is that they have made the decision to make their lives better.

Napoleon Hill, author of the classic *Think and Grow Rich*, has noted that successful people make decisions quickly and firmly once they have reviewed all of the information available. Unsuccessful people, he said, make decisions slowly and change them often. He claimed also that ninety-eight out of every one hundred people never make up their minds about their major purpose in life because *they simply can't make a decision and stick with it*. I hope to help you become one of those people who can make good life decisions.

■ Decisions, Decisions, Decisions

We all make decisions every day. Unfortunately, most of us fail to recognize how important it is that we do our best to make good decisions. To make good decisions, you need to assess your personal strengths, needs, and resources, then check them against your rules of the road.

Identify a good decision you have made for yourself.

_____

_____

_____

Now refer back to the list of characteristics of good and bad decisions. Which characteristics of good decisions does your chosen decision reflect?

_____

_____

_____

Describe a bad decision you have made for yourself.

_____

_____

_____

Which characteristics of bad decisions does this decision reflect?

_____

_____

_____

It's always easy to second-guess yourself. To be successful in life, you need to eliminate that by learning how to think about the consequences of your decisions before you make them. Here, write down a decision you need to make, then use the list of characteristics of good and bad decisions to help you decide what to do. Remember this: it's often harder to make the best decision, but the long-term results of good decisions will always outweigh the short-term benefits of bad ones.

I need to decide . . .

_____

_____

Based on the characteristics of good and bad decisions, my decision is to . . .

_____

_____

I am deciding to do that because it reflects these characteristics of good decisions:

_____

_____

_____

_____

147

Putting Off Procrastination

One of the biggest obstacles in the decision-making process is something I am very familiar with: procrastination, or the tendency to put things off. I've worked at overcoming my own inclination to procrastinate. Mark Twain is the literary hero of procrastinators. His motto was "Never put off till tomorrow what you can do the day after tomorrow."

There are two types of procrastinators: the *arousal* type and the *avoidance* type. Arousal types put things off because they get a thrill out of doing things in a last-minute rush and at the buzzer. If you put off writing papers and doing assignments until the last moment, you know a little something about this type of procrastination. The second type puts things off to avoid them for various reasons, ranging from fear of failure to wanting to avoid unpleasant things. Those who procrastinate because they have a fear of failure believe that they are better off not trying than trying and failing. They don't realize that not to try is the biggest failure of all.

Understanding Procrastinators

Procrastinators come in all shapes and sizes, but here are a few common phrases you'll hear from serious procrastinators:

- This isn't the right time to make that decision
- I have a few other things to deal with first
- I don't have time for that
- I've been meaning to get to that
- I'll do that when I've got more experience
- You wouldn't believe all the stuff I have to do before I can get to that
- Tomorrow
- I'm too distracted to do that
- I'm waiting to make a bigger move
- There is probably a safer (better, faster, easier) way of doing this. I'll wait for it

Decision-making gridlock is a serious problem if you are interested in pursuing your vision for a better life. Often, it is based in fear—of success or of failure or simply of pulling your head out of the ground. Think about the successful people you know. Are any of them procrastinators? Do they spend days looking before they leap? Or do they go after what they want?

Getting Past Procrastination

Here are eight tips to help my fellow procrastinators out there get beyond their "buts" and "one day I'm gonnas."

1. **Take small bites.** It's easy for procrastinators to put off large or complex projects or tasks—they never have enough time to finish it all at once. Therefore, why start? Of course, with this attitude, you'll never finish the task, and it will loom larger and larger over your head until you get quite depressed or feel frantic about it.

   Think in terms of one of those Mexican restaurants that advertises "burritos as big as your head." They aren't exaggerating much. But you don't order one and then say, "I think I'll wait for a better time to eat this." No—you get to work on it. You don't try to do it in one huge bite, however; you eat that giant burrito one small bite at a time. And one small bite at a time is not only good for digestion, it is also good for decision-making. Tackle your tasks and decisions one manageable piece at a time.

2. **Begin now!** Without giving yourself time to think of excuses, sit down now and start the process. Force yourself to keep at it for at least an hour. If you choose to stop, set a time to pick up where you left off. This is a critical point, because one thing procrastinators aren't slow with is excuses. If you force yourself to do something *immediately,* you may surprise yourself at how pleased you are with the progress you make. It may even inspire you to keep at it a little at a time until you finish.

3. **Slam the door on critics.** If you feel that you can't make a decision because someone is holding you back, break free of that sense of helplessness and victimization. Sometimes you have to go against the opinions of those around you in order to make the right decisions for yourself. You can't expect others to always share your vision. So, don't let anything or anyone stand between you and your freedom to make decisions that improve your life. It is simply impossible to always reach a consensus.

4. **Lighten up.** Procrastinators tend to take themselves far too seriously. The world is not focused on your every move. The stars will still shine tonight. The sun will still come up tomorrow. No matter what you do, the future of the galaxy is not resting on your shoulders. If the thought of making a decision is weighing so heavily that you can't make it, you need to step away and regain perspective so that you are not taking yourself so seriously. Do something to take your mind off of it and to lighten your mood.

5. **Think of the carrot, not the stick.** Those who put things off sometimes do it because they focus on the difficulties and demands of taking an action rather than on the rewards that await them. How many times have you worried about doing something only to discover that it was not nearly as painful as you had imagined? Always keep in mind the rewards of taking action; don't focus so much on the problems of

taking action that you are frozen in fear. When you make a decision that will be challenging for you to carry out but will better your life, keep in mind how that action will ultimately reward you. If you lose that focus, you might lose your desire to act.

6. **Bring in a coach.** These days, people have personal fitness trainers, personal bankers, personal speech coaches, personal accountants, personal nutrition advisors. Why not bring in a friend or family member to be your antiprocrastination coach? Give your coach a list of the things you need to do and order him or her to keep on you until you do them. Provide the whip if you feel it is necessary. Chronic procrastination calls for drastic action.

7. **Live in the moment.** Use up every minute, every hour, every day, until you have made the most of your entire life. Be guided in your decisions by your vision for your life. When you have no vision, you have no real focus, and it's easy to waste time. With vision, however, you can choose to live in the moment, doing things with a purpose in mind, all leading toward making that vision reality.

8. **Don't demand perfection.** Tell yourself that there is never going to be a *perfect* time to get started and that you don't have to be *perfect* in your performance. Compromise and start immediately. Rough out the task and then build upon it. No one is standing over your shoulder demanding that you make no mistakes.

▪ "Mañana . . ."

Mañana is Spanish for "tomorrow," which is the procrastinator's favorite word. For procrastinators, tomorrow is the perfect time to start something. "Tomorrow!" is the procrastinator's battle cry.

Are *you* a procrastinator? If you put off doing this worksheet until tomorrow, we'll know you are. (Just kidding . . .) Answer the following questions to check your "procrastination rating."

When faced with a large or complex task, you . . .
a. Hide behind the couch until the task deadline has passed
b. Consider all the things you have to do to complete the task and get depressed
c. Make a game plan and then begin bit by bit

You have just been assigned to write a five-page paper for one of your classes. You react by . . .
a. Going to a fast-food restaurant because you can think better on a full stomach
b. Asking your friends what they are going to write about
c. Getting a start on your paper, even if it's to research what topic you want to write about

When you are in the middle of a project or task, and someone laughs and says, "Man, no way can *you* do that!," you . . .

a. Agree with the person and say you must have had sunstroke when you took on the task

b. Say you could do it if you wanted, but you guess you didn't really want to do it right now

c. Tell the person to go take a hike, because this is important to you and you're going to do it

When a task appears to be larger than the world to you, you tell yourself . . .

a. That indeed it is monumental, and the whole of humankind depends on you to accomplish this unattainable task, and thus all is gloom and misery, and there is no meaning to life anymore

b. That you know it's really not that big, but it *feels* that big, and you're still stuck and gloomy

c. That you're not performing brain surgery or curing cancer; the world—and you—will go on regardless of how you perform in this task

When faced with a difficult task, you tend to focus on . . .

a. The girl or boy you'd like to go out with

b. The difficulties involved, until they seem overwhelming

c. The rewards at the end, which are tied directly to the purpose of doing the task in the first place

Because you have a history of procrastinating, you think it's a good idea for future tasks that you have some outside support and encouragement. Therefore, you . . .

a. Contact your local Procrastinators Anonymous organization, only to find out that their next meeting has been postponed

b. Enlist the support of your best friend, who is one of the founding members of your local Procrastinators Anonymous

c. Ask a friend or family member to hold you accountable and to help keep you on track

When you hear the phrase "Seize the day!," you think of . . .

a. The battle cry of South American revolutionaries

b. People who take on life with a zest, voraciously eating it up and looking for more, and you decide that fairly soon, when the time is right, you are going to be like that, too

c. How you can make the most of every day, living with a purpose in mind and making decisions according to that purpose

You are faced with a difficult challenge and you find yourself in a familiar place: stuck. You realize that your expectations for yourself are too high and are the reason you're stuck. You decide to

a. Give up and pretend you didn't care about the challenge in the first place

b. Wait until you have a little more time to tackle the challenge head on

c. Ease up on your expectations and not expect perfection, because you know you won't do anything otherwise

If you answered mainly a's or b's, you are a seasoned procrastinator and need to work on the eight points for getting past procrastination. If you answered mainly c's, you don't have problems with procrastination; you can make decisions and get to the task at hand. Congratulations!

Making Good Decisions a Habit

Before I introduce my decision-making process to you, I want to get you thinking about your own decision-making habits. You probably haven't given much thought to them because you make so many decisions in your life—when to get up, what to have for breakfast, and so on—that the process has become automatic.

Larger decisions, though, aren't so automatic: You want to commit to a relationship but you've been burned before and are wary. You want to try out for a team or for a role in a play, but you don't want to embarrass yourself. You are considering taking a difficult class that you think will help you in the future but you're not so sure you can do well in it.

To make difficult decisions wisely, it helps to have a process for assessing each alternative and its consequences. Such a process will help you make decisions that are consistent with your values and principles as well as with your vision for a better life. It is also vital that you identify and evaluate as many alternatives as possible when making a decision. You also need to be prepared to handle criticism, which will often accompany a decision to make a change.

The amount of time and effort you invest in making a particular decision depends on how important and how difficult the decision is. Even with important decisions, however, many people too often follow the same casual process they use in daily decision-making. They don't open their minds to all of the alternatives that may be available to them, and they don't think through all of the possible ramifications of each alternative.

▪ Learning from Your Past

Think back now and list three big decisions you have made in the last few years. They don't necessarily have to be *good* decisions—just three of the *biggest* decisions you have made.

Over the last few years my three biggest decisions have included:

1. _____

2. _____

3. _____

What made these decisions *big*? The expense they involved? The amount of time they consumed? The changes they required you to make in your lifestyle or attitude? The risks involved?

Next to each of those decisions, write down why they were so significant:

The Decision   **The Significance**

1. _____   _____

   _____   _____

2. _____   _____

   _____   _____

3. _____   _____

   _____   _____

In looking back at these decisions and all that was involved in them, how do you feel now about the decisions you made? Did you make good decisions or bad ones? Note below whether each decision proved to be good or bad, and why.

The Decision   **It was good/bad because:**

1. _____   _____

   _____   _____

2. _____   _____

   _____   _____

3. _____   _____

   _____   _____

Now, think about *how* you made those big decisions, the process you used. Was it the same process you normally use in making your smaller daily decisions or was it a more complex, thoughtful process? How did you arrive at your decision?

The Decision	I decided to do this because:
1._____	_____
_____	_____
2._____	_____
_____	_____
3._____	_____
_____	_____

From your list, choose the most difficult decision you made. Try to recall all of the alternatives you considered before making the decision.

The decision I faced was . . .

_____

_____

_____

The alternatives I considered included . . .

_____

_____

_____

Now that some time has passed, were there any alternatives that you did not consider but now, in retrospect, think you should have included in the process of making the decision? If so, what were they?

_____

_____

_____

Note what criticisms you were subjected to because of the decision you made. Next to each, write down its source.

The Criticism	The Critic
_____	_____
_____	_____
_____	_____

How did you feel about this criticism? How did you respond to it?

_____

_____

_____

Would your response be different today? If so, how?

_____

_____

_____

Using Logic, Emotions, and a Positive Outlook

Some people like to make decisions based on pure logic, using only their minds. Others go more on feel, deciding based on their emotional response. Important matters require that you use *both* your mind and your heart. Don't rely only on logic and put aside your emotions, or vice versa, when it comes to making big decisions in your life.

Even after you have intellectually weighed a decision, there remains the matter of what you feel in your heart. Some call this your "gut instinct." It is an instinct based on past experiences and the emotional value you place on the decision.

There is one more aspect of decision-making that you need to consider before I introduce you to my process: I am going to ask you to smile while you go through it. Science once scoffed at the notion that a positive attitude could seriously affect your physical and mental health, but not anymore. Negative thinking can cripple you mentally, spiritually, and physically, and it can also impede your ability to make decisions wisely. An optimistic and positive emotional approach to decision-making, on the other hand, helps you to consider all the factors involved.

The Winning-by-a-Decision Process

Now, finally, I'll present my process for making big decisions. I like to use boxing as a metaphor for the process, which is split into five steps:

1. The weigh-in
2. Suiting up

3. Checking the fit
4. Stepping into the ring
5. Going for the knockout

Step One: The Weigh-In

Big decisions often are spurred by your learning something that sheds new light or gives you a new perspective on an existing situation. This new information or perspective forces you to examine your situation and to weigh the possibilities of making a change.

The key questions to consider at this stage in the decision-making process are 1.) Are the risks serious if I don't change? And 2.) Do the benefits of changing outweigh the risks involved?

If the risks in your current behavior or situation aren't serious, then continuing on your current path is a workable option. Likewise, if the benefits of changing don't outweigh the risks involved in making the change, you might also consider staying on your current path. If, however, staying on your current path is risky, or if the benefits you would reap by making a change outweigh the risks involved in making the change, then you would be better off making the change.

Step Two: Suiting Up

The next step in the decision-making process is to identify as many suitable alternative solutions or courses of actions as possible. This is another stop in the Success Process where it is useful to let your imagination run wild, to dream up as many possible solutions as you can, weigh them all, and pick and choose those that might appear to work.

The more information you have about an issue, the more you consider the issue from various perspectives as objectively as possible, the better you can decide what's best for you. Be open to all alternatives at this stage, even if some appear to be a bit wild. Sometimes we need to step outside of our boxes and consider things that appear to be unlikely solutions. Many times the greatest decisions are those that make you stray far from the beaten path.

Step Three: Checking the Fit

Once you have identified suitable alternatives, the next step is to mentally try each one on and check to see which best fits your vision for a better life. Carefully examine each alternative, get a feel for them, and evaluate the pros and cons of each. Examine them for both the short term and the long term—and realize that short-term benefits might appear enticing, but they can come at the expense of greater long-term benefits. If you don't find any alternatives that match up with your vision for a better life, you may have to go back to step two and come up with more attractive alternatives.

The key questions that need to be answered at this stage are which alternative is best and whether the best alternative will help you meet your goals.

Step Four: Stepping into the Ring

At this point, you are like an actor taking on a role. After identifying the alternative—or alternatives, if you are torn between a number of choices—imagine yourself taking a particular course and consider the implications. What might happen if you take this route with your life? What will the effect be on your personal development and relationships, your future career, your place in the community? Will it move you along toward your vision for a better life?

Sometimes, of course, you may have to take a side road in your journey through the Success Process. Regardless of the situation, when you walk into the ring mentally with each alternative, always keep your ultimate goal in mind.

As you try out the most appealing alternatives, you will develop a sense of which is the best choice for you, and, without even realizing it, you will move closer to making a final decision. Now, the key question is whether to make a decision—whether to pursue this change.

Step Five: Go for the Knockout!

Once you have committed to making a decision that you have carefully evaluated, you should be prepared to take it all the way without retreating. Know that there will be times when your decision will be challenged, but if you have followed each step in the process and given careful thought to your choices along the way, you should be able to face these challenges and overcome them.

■ The Decision Process

You've just read about the five steps to making good decisions:

1. The weigh-in
2. Suiting up
3. Checking the fit
4. Stepping into the ring
5. Going for the knockout

Now take the time to work through a decision of your own, using this process.

■ Step One: The Weigh-In

Write down a decision that you are currently facing. (*Note: Choose an issue for which you feel the benefits outweigh the risks—otherwise, you have no need to go on to step two!*)

_____

_____

_____

What are the risks you face if you decide not to change your situation? Are they serious risks? Write them below:

_____

_____

_____

What are the benefits of making the change?

_____

_____

_____

Do the benefits you've just identified outweigh the risks?

_____

_____

_____

_____

■ Step Two: Suiting Up

Explore the alternatives that you can choose among in making the best decision. Be creative; think of as many solutions as you can.

_____

_____

_____

_____

_____

_____

■ Step Three: Checking the Fit

An effective way to check the fit of each alternative is to create a Decision Balance Sheet. In the space below, write down one alternative from step 2 that appears to be strong:

_____

_____

Now, list the pros and cons of this alternative in each category listed.

How will this affect your personal development?

Pros   **Cons**

_____   _____

_____   _____

_____   _____

_____   _____

_____   _____

159

How will this affect your future career?

Pros	Cons
_____	_____
_____	_____
_____	_____
_____	_____
_____	_____

How will this affect your relationships?

Pros	Cons
_____	_____
_____	_____
_____	_____
_____	_____

Now, review the pros and cons in each area of your life. When you find one on each side that appears to balance each other out, cross the pair out. If you find one pro that seems equal to two cons, cross all three out. If you find two cons equal to three pros, cross out all five. Do this with every possible alternative until you determine whether its impact on your life would be positive or negative overall. This is a subjective way of measuring a decision's appeal to you; if nothing else, it makes you thoroughly think through each alternative.

Note that there are two types of errors that commonly arise in completing the balance sheet:

1. You may overlook cons because you are reluctant to admit the potential for negative results
2. You may be overly optimistic in projecting pros

Remember that this has to be a thoroughly honest process; otherwise it is invalid. By being candid and thoughtful at this stage, you can save yourself a great deal of regret down the road.

▨ Step Four: Stepping into the Ring

Now imagine that you have identified the best decision alternative after weighing the pros and cons of all of your choices, and answer these questions.

What impact will pursuing this alternative have on your personal development?

_____

_____

_____

. . . on your future career?

_____

_____

_____

. . . on your relationships?

_____

_____

_____

How will this decision to change move you toward your vision for a better life?

_____

_____

_____

Making decisions can be a difficult process, but mastering the process is essential to your ability to shape your life and move toward your vision. And the decision-making process is one that is closely connected to the topic in the final step: that of committing to your vision. Decisions and commitments are intertwined. Good decisions can help you stay committed to your vision even in the face of adversity.

Step 9: Commit to Your Vision

Things do not happen; things are made to happen.

—John F. Kennedy

You've come a long way in learning the Success Process. Through the first eight steps, you've learned how to:

- Be more self-aware and know what your gifts and talents are
- Create your vision for your life
- Develop plans that will help make your vision happen
- Employ some rules of the road to keep you on track
- Take the risks necessary to move forward
- Adapt to change and make change work *for* you rather than *against* you
- Use teamwork and the support of others to adapt to changes and to reach your goals
- Shape your life through wise decisions

The final piece to the puzzle is commitment to your vision. You surely will be tested along the way, and without commitment, you won't be able to overcome the challenges and obstacles that you will face.

There is great power in making a commitment to bettering your life. When you dedicate yourself to rising above your circumstances, you will rise. When you let the people around you know that you not only *want* something better, but you are *dedicated* to it as well, they buy into your vision for yourself. They become your cheerleaders and champions.

Why is it that we cheer the underdogs in sporting events and movies? Why do the benchwarmers who play with enthusiasm draw cheers as great as those given the stars when they enter a game? Because the fans sense a *commitment* to the game in those players too. They want to reward that commitment. That is part of the human spirit. We appreciate and want to see those who strive succeed.

That success often only comes with firm commitment. In this chapter, you'll learn how to:

- Commit to bettering your life
- Create positive energy from your commitments
- Honor your commitments
- Pursue your vision with enthusiasm
- Make commitments part of your everyday life

Committing to Bettering Your Life

Committing to bettering your life means never giving up, never giving in, never losing your focus and your desire to better yourself, whether in your relationships or personal development, your education or career, or your role as a positive force in your community.

All the other steps directly affect your commitment. Consider:

- Knowing who you are and what your talents and gifts are will help you stay committed to bettering your life and using those talents and gifts
- Your vision and your plan act as anchors when the winds of trouble want to blow you away
- Having your rules of the road in place helps you to find and keep your way
- Taking risks to move forward and adapting to change would be awfully hard to do without a firm commitment to your vision
- A support team can offer encouragement and advice and help you stay committed

All of these steps work together to make your vision happen.

What does it mean to make a commitment? It means persevering and holding on to your dreams and goals no matter how difficult the circumstances. It means valuing and believing in your vision more than you fear the dangers and obstacles that await you. It means focusing on your vision and taking necessary risks because you are worth it and deserve a better life.

When you are committed to your vision, you have to *expect* good things to happen—no matter what the odds, no matter what logic whispers in your ear, no matter what other people might tell you. Had David listened to logic and to the people around him, he would never have had the courage or the boldness to challenge Goliath. No one expected David to be victorious; all counsel said to avoid confrontation. But David had a very different vision and a total commitment to that vision. He acted on that vision and he accomplished the unbelievable.

David was just a young person, flesh and blood, just like you. Things are no different for you: you have a choice, just as David did. You can live in fear and shrink back at challenges, like the other Israelites, or you can step up, fully committed to your vision, like David did.

You can do amazing things when you are committed to doing them. Notice I *don't* say you can achieve whatever you want easily. You need to be committed for the very reason that achievement *won't* come easily. But if you want it, and you have a wise plan in place, and you follow the plan and take well-considered risks and adapt to change and lean on others when you need to, you can make it. You can do it if you're committed to doing it.

▪ Committing to Bettering Your Life

Keeping Commitments

Write down some commitments you have made already in your life, such as your commitment to your family, to your friends, to a relationship, to sports or other pursuits, to a social cause, or to a career path.

I have committed to:

_____

_____

_____

_____

_____

Next, for each commitment that you have *kept*, note the positive results that have come from keeping that commitment.

Commitment Kept   **Result**

_____   _____

_____   _____

_____   _____

Now, note some commitments that you have not been able to keep.

_____

_____

_____

_____

Why were you not able to keep these commitments? Be honest with yourself; you can only learn from your past when you're honest about it.

_____

_____

_____

_____

What was the result of not being able to keep these commitments?

_____

_____

_____

_____

Write down some small commitments that you can make in the coming days and weeks to help you build your power to keep commitments. For example, commit to reading an inspiring book about someone such as Nelson Mandela, who committed his life to freeing his nation from apartheid, or Martin Luther King Jr., who fought for civil rights and changed this nation just as Mandela changed his.

In the next week, I commit to three actions that will move me closer to my vision of a better life:

1. _____

2. _____

3. _____

Creating Positive Energy from Your Commitments

The commitments in your life clearly have a great impact on the quality of life you lead. Being committed to goals and principles and to living a better life creates positive energy that affects all areas of your life.

You can't fake commitment. You either put everything into it or you don't. Have you ever witnessed a game in which someone competing wasn't really committed to winning? It wasn't hard to pick that person out, was it? That person may have *thought* he was committed to playing and winning, but his actions told the truth.

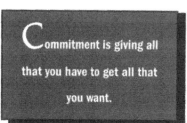
Commitment is giving all that you have to get all that you want.

Commitment is giving all that you have to get all that you want. Many people who are unhappy with their lives or circumstances miss this point—they seem to think the answer is to complain. But what good does it do to attack a negative situation with negative attitudes and behavior? That approach reflects a *victim mentality*. People who adopt this attitude blame. They foster resentment and anger. And they just don't get it.

Nobody cheers for a player with a bad attitude. Bosses don't look to promote the worker who complains or does a tough job poorly. The world in general does not respond to negative energy.

Commitment is setting goals and working your hardest to attain them. That capacity can be enlarged only through exercising your power to make commitments and fulfill them. When you make and keep commitments, you will create a positive energy that will make it easier and easier to keep future commitments. You will begin to realize that you *can* do what you set out to do. This will propel you to greater and greater achievements.

■ Commit to Your Vision

This activity helps you focus on past commitments and whether they were successful or not, and then make new or renewed commitments.

Fill out the following chart, focusing on commitments you have made in each Success Circle over the past six months (see the Success Circles in Chapter 1, "The Success Process"). In addition to listing a commitment made for each circle, write whether or not you were successful in keeping that commitment, and why. If you failed in the commitment, state what you could have done to be successful.

Success Circle: Personal Development Commitment	Success Circle: Career Commitment	Success Circle: Relationships Commitment
Successful? Yes No	Successful? Yes No	Successful? Yes No
If not successful, what could you have done to be successful?	If not successful, what could you have done to be successful?	If not successful, what could you have done to be successful?

Now repeat the process, but instead of identifying past commitments, identify a commitment within each Success Circle that you will make now, and explain what you will do to keep that commitment successfully.

Success Circle: Personal Development Commitment	Success Circle: Career Commitment	Success Circle: Relationships Commitment
What will you do to be successful?	What will you do to be successful?	What will you do to be successful?

Honoring Your Commitments

Keeping a commitment is a major step forward, but breaking one is a step back. Don't make commitments that you can't keep, because if you do, you will never advance toward your vision of a better life. Make commitments wisely and only after careful consideration. If you overload yourself with responsibilities, you will succeed only in frustrating yourself and those around you.

When you keep your commitments, you build trust in yourself and with others. Commitments are promises, and each commitment that you make and stick with is a goal achieved. Each goal that you achieve is another indication that you are guided by the possibilities of your life rather than the circumstances.

Too many people give only lip service to "making a commitment." They mentally embrace the idea without performing the action. Making a commitment means devoting your time and effort to achieving objectives: taking action. Commitments can be very broad and involve virtually all aspects of your life, such as a commitment to live a more healthy life. They can also be very specific, such as a commitment to earn all A's and B's this semester, or to earn an A in a particular class. Each commitment, however, is directed toward achieving *results,* regardless of whether it is general or specific.

Pursuing Your Vision with Enthusiasm

To be committed, you have to have goals, but you also must have vision and *enthusiasm* about avidly pursuing that vision. As Emerson put it, "Nothing great is ever achieved without enthusiasm."

Think about the people you know who seem to be just going through the motions. What do they have in common? They lack direction. They have no enthusiasm. The thought of a challenge sends them fleeing in terror back to their La-Z-Boy recliners, back to the television, back to the street-corner hangout, back to a life going nowhere fast.

Now, think about the people you know who are full of life. What do they all share? A purpose and direction. An enthusiasm for life. A joy in what they are doing. A willingness to face challenges and overcome them. Being mentally and emotionally committed to enthusiastically pursuing your vision for a better life is vital for five reasons.

1. **You can meet challenges.** You can respond in one of two ways when your vision for a better life is challenged: you can give up or you can step up. If you are enthusiastic and committed to bettering your life, you'll step up and accept challenges as opportunities for growth. If you are uncommitted, you'll retreat. Enthusiasm helps you overcome obstacles in your path along the Success Process.

2. **You can develop your talents.** When you are committed and enthusiastic, you make it possible for all of your talents to be developed and put to their highest use. That is accomplished only by commitment and enthusiasm, by constantly striving to tap into the deepest reserves, pulling out all that is within you and unleashing those gifts granted you.

3. **You can rev up for risks.** Emotional commitment will rev you up to take the risks that you need to take. Without that commitment, you can't see the value of taking risks, and, therefore, you are not willing to make the leap. If you don't put your heart into your pursuit of a better life, you won't be willing to take the risks that are essential.

4. **You can develop excellence.** When you are enthusiastically committed to your vision, you make it possible for your gifts to stand out and for you to excel. It often is this commitment to excellence that distinguishes those who are truly committed from those who want something but aren't willing to put forth the effort to achieve it.

5. **You can inspire others to help you.** The enthusiasm and passion you bring to a commitment inspire excellence. Excellence in turn inspires others to care about your commitment. When you bring passion to your commitment, you inspire others to share your vision and to look for ways to help you. Your enthusiasm is the match that lights the fire of commitment in you and in those around you.

Making Commitments Part of Your Everyday Life

In your commitment to pursue a better life, three types of commitments are essential. Make these commitments part of your everyday life; weave them into your thoughts and actions. The commitments are:

- Celebrating your successes
- Helping others pursue a better life
- Continuously learning and growing

Celebrating Your Success

At first glance, you may think this sounds silly. Who wouldn't celebrate success when it comes? The truth is, however, that people often are not prepared for success. Sometimes they feel undeserving of success, unworthy of it, and they can't handle it. They self-destruct.

Commit to success by earning it and knowing that you deserve it. Prepare yourself so that when success comes, you are comfortable with it. Learn to celebrate your successes and acknowledge your defeats, and then move on to the next opportunity and challenge. Celebrating success doesn't mean you coast or put your drive into neutral; it simply means that you acknowledge your effort and your accomplishment, you take joy and pride in it. Note, too, that pride doesn't mean you thump your chest and crow about your achievements; it means that you value your gifts and accomplishments. You appreciate them for what they are. Celebrating success is a healthy way of life.

Helping Others

Along with committing to your own success, commit also to helping others, particularly those who are struggling, to find their own way to success. You don't have to wait until you are on top to consider your role in your community. Look around you. You can help people right now. You can help by offering encouragement and support. You can be there for friends. You can join a mentoring program for grade school kids. You can make a pact with a friend and hold him or her accountable to goals. You can join in community projects and activities, raising money for causes that you believe in. You can tutor someone in a favorite subject area. You can volunteer for student committees or for nonprofit organizations or for hospitals or nursing homes within your community. You have plenty to offer to the people around you—your friends, your peers, your community—right now.

Continuously Learning and Growing

If you want to be successful and maintain success, you have to commit to a lifetime of learning and growing. Learning refers not only to formal education, but to self-education: reading, traveling, exploring new fields, new training, and continuous personal, spiritual, and intellectual learning. The U.S. Department of Education reports that most adults will have at least three significant job changes in their lifetime. That means you will need to keep your mind sharp by continuously developing your ability to absorb new information while building your emotional and spiritual strength to handle all that life throws at you.

Reading as much as you can find about your areas of interest will open up your world. You might not get to where you want to be in your life if you don't make the effort to find out how to get there by reading and learning.

You grow by constantly renewing your commitment to bettering yourself in each of your Success Circles. Why should you strive to grow even after you have achieved a goal? Because that is what makes for a dynamic and rewarding life. Why sit on the sidelines of life if you can challenge yourself to develop your talents and skills even more? Why not take it all the way to the wall, using up every ounce of energy, every bit of creativity, every resource that the universe provides?

What will your list of accomplishments be at the end of your life? Will it be a long list? Listen to that inner voice and cultivate it. Use the steps in the Success Process as guides for pursuing a better life that forever follows the upward spiral.

▪ Committing to Excellence

Success is found through the pursuit of excellence. It is tied in to your personal development as well as to your relationships with others. Answer the following questions to help you make a commitment to excellence.

How can you commit to helping others pursue a better life? Be as specific as possible—if you'd like, name a particular person you could help.

_____

_____

_____

_____

How will helping others help you in your own pursuit of a better life?

_____

_____

_____

We all need to grow throughout our lives. Identify some ways you can continue your growth spiritually, intellectually, and emotionally.

Spiritual growth

_____

_____

_____

Intellectual growth

_____

_____

_____

Emotional growth

_____

Look around you at the temptations and the distractions of the modern world. Think about how easy it is to give in to those negative influences. Why not just kick back and go where life takes you? Why not give in to all the seductions of tobacco and alcohol, drugs and crime? Why should you commit to bettering your life?

The answer is simple: if you don't stick up for you, who will? If you don't pursue your vision of a better life, who is going to pursue it for you? If you choose to settle for less than what is possible for your life, you have no one else to blame but yourself for what you get. If you fall into a downward spiral through drugs or crime, will the world cheer you on? Or will you suffer the consequences of your own laziness and lack of commitment?

Do you want the good life? Follow the Success Process, and even the worst days will be better than the best days you'll have in the downward spiral. Why? Because when you follow the Success Process, *you* are in control of your life. You decide where you are going, when you are going, and how you are going to get there. You are in control. A better life is always within your power to achieve.

Life is only as good as you make it, so make your life a good one and enjoy your journey. Good luck—and remember: you *can* make it happen.

About the Author

STEDMAN GRAHAM is chairman and chief executive officer of S. Graham & Associates, an educational company that creates customized corporate-training and leadership-development programs. He is also the author of several books, including the *New York Times* best-sellers *You Can Make It Happen* and *Teens Can Make It Happen,* both of which detail his philosophy for personal growth. His other books include *You Can Make It Happen Every Day* and *Build Your Own Life Brand!*

A commitment to youth and community is central to Stedman Graham's philosophy. He is the founder of The Leadership Institute of Chicago and a member of the National Board of Junior Achievement. He is also an adjunct professor at the Kellogg Graduate School of Management at Northwestern University, a distinguished visiting professor at Coker College, and a visiting professor at George Washington University. Graham received a bachelor's degree in social work from Hardin-Simmons University and earned a master's degree in education from Ball State University.

Made in the USA
Lexington, KY
19 August 2015